MASSACRE AT HILL 303

MASSACRE
AT HILL 303

Basil B. Clark with James Melvin Rudd

To Brittany stept
.a good therpast

James Melvin Rudd

Deeds Publishing | Atlanta

Published by Deeds Publishing in Athens, GA
www.deedspublishing.com

Printed in The United States of America

Cover design and text layout by Mark Babcock

Library of Congress Cataloging-in-Publications data is available upon request.

ISBN 978-1-947309-27-2

Books are available in quantity for promotional or premium use. For information, email info@deedspublishing.com.

First Edition, 2018

10 9 8 7 6 5 4 3 2 1

Foreword

The 1st Cavalry Division was formed on September 13, 1921 at Fort Bliss, Texas. Ms. Gladys Finch Dorcy, wife of Colonel Ben Dorcy—commander of the 7th Cavalry Regiment at the time—was the creator of the Division's patch. When asked why the patch was so big—still the biggest in the U.S. Army today—she answered "the patch had to be seen through the dust and sand at Fort Bliss, and we made it that way because it is worn by big men who do big things." Hundreds of thousands of courageous men and women have worn the iconic "1st Cav" patch since 1921, distinguishing themselves in tough combat including World War II, the Korean War, the Vietnam War, Operation Desert Storm, and most recently the Global War on Terror. Ms. Dorcy was absolutely right, those that have had the honor of wearing the 1st Cav patch have indeed done "big things", keeping the gates of freedom open on our behalf.

James Melvin Rudd is one of those "big men". So is Basil B. Clark. Two combat infantry veterans that fought in different wars at different times at different locations, but bonded by their shared service in the 1st Cavalry Division. During a chance meeting at a Veterans Affairs medical clinic in 2014, Vietnam War veteran Basil Clark, noticed Korean War veteran James Rudd in the waiting area. Both were wearing hats with 1st Cavalry insignia, so a special conversation was struck; a conversation that only combat veterans could have, and in this case, only 1st Cavalry combat veterans.

What followed that initial conversation is a gripping record of an infantryman's perspective of the Korean War, *Massacre at Hill 303*. As told to Basil Clark, with great trust and clarity, James Rudd shares powerful and poignant memories from his life, centered on intense combat during the Korean War. It begins with James Rudd's trying times in childhood, but marked by a penchant to serve in the military. He managed to enlist before he was of legal age, shortly after World War II when our military was drastically downsizing and not ready for major conflict. Little did James Rudd realize that he would be part of the vanguard into a vicious war on the Korean peninsula, a war that our military was not prepared to wage. However, he willingly put his life on the line and valiantly dealt with the rigors and challenges.

The horrors of war and the rawness of combat transformed him from an innocent adolescent to a hardened combat veteran. It caused him to question his values, but he maintained his sterling character, and even later forgave. As with other warriors that make it home from combat, James Rudd also questions why he survived while many of his close comrades did not. Difficult introspection that the reader can only imagine, but one for which he should have no guilt, especially given that he returned not once, but twice to the front lines from wounds and trauma.

James Rudd is a humble and selfless servant. He did not serve for money, easy work, or glory. Rather, he chose to be a part of something larger than himself, and did so exceedingly well. He served out of love for his country, his family, and for his fellow Soldiers.

He was asked to pack his duffle bags and move out, and he did so with no questions asked. He lived words like duty, honor, and country. He experienced words like hunger, fatigue, and death. On battlefields far from home, he exemplified words like courage, compassion, and loyalty. It is because of men like him, and also Basil Clark, that we enjoy our cherished American way of life. Instead of reading about history, they made history.

Massacre at Hill 303 is a powerful story, frightening at times, heartwarming at times, humorous at times. It is told from a "bottom up" perspective, taking you into the minds of the young service members that do our Nation's bidding. It also provides tremendous insight into the human aspect of warfare, reminding us that wars are ultimately a human endeavor and bring out the good and bad in mankind.

Soldiers that serve together in combat form timeless bonds. These bonds further extend from generation to generation of veterans. In the case of *Massacre at Hill 303,* these special bonds come out front and center. Admirably, several of James Rudd's children and even grandchildren have continued to serve our Nation in uniform. I was recently privileged to command the 1st Cavalry Division, leading them into combat in Afghanistan. Our troopers were fond of saying "Live the Legend". For James Rudd and Basil Clark, they both clearly "Lived the Legend", in fine Cavalry fashion.

—John C. Thomson III
Major General, U.S. Army

Prologue

When I felt the blood on my forehead, my first thought was, *I'm dying*. Two of my buddies had already been hit and were lying catty-cornered atop me, their faces touching mine.

James shuddered as he continued, "I can feel their faces now."

My life was saved because the bullets went through them first. The boy on my left side was lying so that part of his head covered me. I knew when each of them died because there was a change in the way their bodies laid across me. Blood was running over my forehead, but I could still see a little bit from my right eye. I thought I was hit, and so I barely started to reach my left arm to see how badly, but in a split second I came to my senses and thought, Melvin, don't move your hand anymore and you might be thought dead.

My thoughts flashed back to a time when I was little and walking the railroad tracks near our house. There was a man and woman in the neighborhood, Clayton and Polly, they weren't married, but they lived together. Polly always carried a pistol. They owned a bar joint and for some reason were arguing. Well, I saw that Polly was walking down the railroad tracks away from their place,

1

and Clayton started after her. When he caught up with her she pulled her .38 Special out of her purse. Clayton quickly pulled his pistol and shot her in the front lobe. She survived and lived for some time after that.

And, lying there, blood flowing over my forehead in that dried out rice paddy, I thought, I don't know how bad I'm hit, but if Polly could live after she was shot in the head, I can too. If you don't move, Melvin, maybe you'll be left for dead, and then you can try and escape.

I know the boys lying atop me were hit at least seven times after the initial round of shooting because I felt their bodies jerking each time a bullet hit. Sometimes I can't seem to get away from that feeling; lying there, knowing I couldn't do anything, hoping and praying that somehow I would survive.

1. To Find Out How Something Works

I was born in Salyersville, Kentucky, the first of six children, to James Earl and Ethel Mae Rudd.

James grinned. The doctor that delivered me was an old man that I believe also liked some White Lightning occasionally, and when I was born he messed up my birth certificate. He got it mixed up with another baby he delivered the same day, Florence Owens. I got all that straightened out when I joined the Army.

I was young; I'm not sure how old maybe five or six, when my father decided that to find work we would have to move to Michigan. A while after we moved there, my dad started a new habit. On a fairly regular basis he would drive by the bus station and if he saw someone that had just gotten off the bus, but seemed confused about what to do next, my father would tell him where he could go to find work.

One time he saw a man that had just gotten off the bus standing on the corner holding only a brown paper bag. My father knew that was probably all he owned in the world, and that he needed help, so he asked him what his name was.

"P. Collins."

"Where are you staying?"

"I don't know."

"Well," my father said, "we have an extra room. It's not much, but you can stay with us for now."

He did, and my dad didn't charge him anything for the room until after he got a job. Mr. P. Collins stayed with us for about two months. In a funny kind of way he put me in mind of Abraham Lincoln, of pictures I'd seen of him that is; he was a tall, lanky man.

He needed a car, and my father had a Model T Ford he wanted to sell.

"How much do you want for that Model T, James?"

"Ten dollars."

P. Collins thought a moment. "I'd like to buy it if you could hold onto it until I have the full ten dollars."

"Tell you what I'll do," my dad said. "You give me what you are able to at this time and the rest of the ten dollars when you get it, and you can have the car now."

P. Collins looked down at his feet a moment and then back up again. "Thank you, James," he quietly said. "I really appreciate it."

Now, to find out how something works, sometimes you have to take it apart, and I was always interested in figuring out how things worked.

The next day, my father and P. Collins were gone to work and P. Collins rode with my dad. I'm not sure why he didn't take the Model T, but anyway, I was a looking at that car, sitting under an old oak tree, I can still see it, and I got to wondering about it, and decided to crawl under it to see if I could figure it out. Now I have to tell you, before I started, I got an empty cardboard box and laid it flat out alongside the Model T. Then I got me some tools and crawled under that car to see if I could make sense of it. First I took the bolts out of the oil pan and carefully put them on that cardboard in the order I disassembled them. The clutch and shift mechanisms were in the same area, under where the seat of the car was, so I got to taking a few things apart there. Now when I put a car part on that cardboard I marked the spot with a pencil carefully so I knew exactly the way things needed to go back.

About the time I had quite a few things spread out alongside that Model T, my father and P. Collins came home from work. P. Collins took one look at that Model T with several of its parts a-laying out beside it and in a high-pitched voice went, "Oo-oo-oo Melvin, you tore my car up! James, look what your boy has done!"

The way he was saying it sounded funny and my dad started laughing. I quickly said I would get it back together, and my father stopped laughing long enough to say, "He will, or I'll set his rear-end on fire!"

P. Collins said, "He'd better, or I want my money back!" My father reassured him that by the time they got home from work the next evening I would have the car back together.

Well the next morning I went back to work on it and when they got home from work the next evening, P. Collins, started up that Model T Ford and it ran perfectly.

I was seven.

2. First Cavalry Veterans

(Basil B. Clark)

The end of February 2014, I was sitting in the VA Outpatient Clinic in Prestonsburg, Kentucky, waiting to be called in for blood work, when a man came in accompanying someone I surmised to be his father. I later found out I was correct. The older gentleman was wearing a hat with 1st Cavalry and Korean War Veteran insignias on it. I had on my hat with its 1st Cavalry and Vietnam Veteran insignias. We each said hello, exchanged names, and then started into conversation, about dates of service, assignments, and the fact that we had both served in the Infantry in combat with the 1st Cavalry Division.

The nurse called my name and I went in to get the necessary needle stick so enough blood could be extracted to fill out the various categories on my blood work chart for the year.

When I went back out to the waiting area, James Rudd was still sitting there. I went to say goodbye, and he asked if I could visit a while. I told him I could, and he continued sharing, including that he had been a prisoner of war during the Korean Conflict. After a few minutes, I told James that I had something for him and went out to my car and got a copy of my book, *War Wounded: Let the Healing Begin*. I signed and gave it to him, at which point he asked what it cost. I told him it was my gift to him, a thanks for his service. We were able to talk quite a bit more as it was another 30-40 minutes before James was called in for his appointment. I had already asked for his address and phone number so we could visit more, so we said our "see you laters;" he went in to keep his doctor's appointment, and I headed back home.

I did call James and coordinated a time to visit him a couple weeks later in his room at Buckingham Place, an assisted living facility in Paintsville, Kentucky. When I called on him, we talked for around three hours, James telling me several stories from his Korean War service, and also stories from his childhood. I told him that his story was compelling and that I would be interested in writing about it.

James said there had been offers to tell his story before but two things stopped him. I believe the first is accurately labeled "Survivor's Guilt." Why should my story be told when it includes so many who lost their lives? The second reason had to do with trust and truth. James said if his story was ever told, he wanted it to be truthful, not something that sounded and read like fiction.

A few weeks later, I was visiting with James again. He had moved from Buckingham Place to Mountain Manor Nursing Home, right across the parking lot. He was in a much smaller room, sharing it with another man, Earl, but James said he wanted to stay with his friend rather than all alone in the larger place.

Again we visited a couple hours before a nurse came by and told James it was time for supper. He replied that he wanted me to join him as his guest, and the nurse said, "Sure."

I was planning on paying for my meal when we came to the desk where a worker sat recording which residents ate in the dining room. James told her, "This is an old friend of mine. He's come a long way to see me, and he's starved to death and he's only got a quarter in his pocket. Can you give him a bite to eat?"

The worker laughed and waved us through. When I told her I'd pay, she said, "No; you're his guest."

We ate our meal and visited some more, and when we were about to leave the dining room, James said he believed he could trust me to tell his story truthfully. I take his trust seriously, and will do my best to honor him.

3. Red Wagons and Comic Books

I guess I was about eight when my mom and I were walking to the store; she went first to Mr. Brown's drugstore, and then the nearby hardware store, I can't quite recall the name of it. Anyway, there was a little red wagon in the window, and I wanted it. Of course, at that age, you have no idea about money, or, in our case, the lack of it.

"Mom, can you buy that red wagon for me?"

"I'd really like to, Melvin, but I don't have the money for it."

"But I really want it!"

"I can't, Melvin."

Well I went to crying and telling her I wanted it, and she was trying her best to get us away from there when the owner of the hardware store came out. I was still a-bawling.

"Is Melvin okay?" he asked.

"Yes, he's just upset because I told him I can't get him that little red wagon."

"I can see that," he said with a bit of a smile. "It *is* something little boys like."

My mother pursed her lips. "How much is it?"

"Nine dollars," he replied.

"Melvin, I've only got two dollars. We don't have enough."

I guess the owner was feeling sorry for us, or wanting to make a sale, or both, probably. Plus he would have known that my dad got paid at the end of the week. "Mrs. Rudd," he said. "If you can give me two dollars now, I'll take your word for the rest."

So, to make a long story short, I went home pulling

that little red wagon behind me. I really did like it, and played with it a lot. I never heard the conversation between my mom and dad about it, but nothing was ever said to me, so I guess it went okay.

There was a Sweet Shop in town that sold liquor, beer, food, gum, candy, comic books; all kinds of stuff. I made a dollar one time and bought me a comic book, and when I brought it home I asked my mother to help me read it, and she did.

When my father got home that night, he said, "No! No comic books!"

"He's learning to read," my mother said, and we kept it. I never heard my father mention it again. But that is how I learned to read. My mother taught me with comic books.

You know, we were poor, but Mom never sent us out with dirty clothes. We may have come back with them dirty, but that's a different story. Patches were okay, but she wasn't going to have folks say she let us out dirty. We had old shoes, but they were clean.

Another thing I remember from around that time. I used to have real curly hair, and I can't remember exactly how old I was, I know we were in Michigan, but I asked my mother to cut it because the girls were teasing me about it and it was embarrassing. She said she understood, and cut it right away.

4. Startling Noises

James looked at me reflectively and said, "I'm going to tell you something that some other young boys and I did when I was in Michigan. Looking back, I wish we hadn't, but we were young, and really didn't know any better."

There was a park not too far from where we lived, and we would go there to play sometimes. One time they were having a celebration for every branch of the service. There was a man in the crowd, from World War I, I think. Now we had heard some people say he was real jumpy around loud, or sudden, noises. Us boys saw him in the crowd and snuck up behind him and clapped our hands all together. Well, he was on a sidewalk that was raised up a little from the rest of the ground, and was there meeting a woman. When we clapped, his immediate reaction was to throw his arms out, and he struck her, and knocked her off the sidewalk. Some police in the area rushed over.

"Hey, buddy, you can't do that! You are under arrest for assaulting that woman!"

Some of the lady's relatives were there, and one of them spoke up. "Officer, please don't arrest that man."

"And just why not?"

Another of her relatives answered, "Because we know that he has been jumpy ever since he came back from war. If you want to arrest anybody, get those kids!"

He didn't get arrested, and neither did we, although we did get a serious talking to. Fortunately, my dad wasn't around, or I'd have gotten a good old thumping on top of that. I don't think anyone ever told him as he never said anything to me about it, and he wasn't the kind of man who would tolerate me doing something like that.

Of course, when I got back from the war, I understood why that boy was so jumpy. I've hit the ground at startling noises a few times in my days, and each time the thought of what we did to that man came back. It was so wrong, just wrong. But like so many things, you can't go back and change anything; you can only hope you learn from it all.

5. My Mother's Death

During one of our visits, I asked James what has been the hardest thing to deal with; he told me when his mother was killed. This caught me off guard as this had not come up in any prior conversations. James elaborated.

I was nine. Her killer was never found, although I have an idea. You know, we were not really accepted when my dad went to Michigan to work. We were considered old hillbillies; some places we even had to go around to the back doors to enter.

James paused reflectively and then continued. I hesitate telling you this, but it's the way it was. My dad was in prison when my mom was killed. He was drinking one night and passed out. A cop handcuffed him while he was still out and then took one of those leather slapjacks they used to carry, still may, I don't know, and anyway he slap jacked my dad. Dad came to and struggled to his feet and the cop told him to get in the car. Dad refused and the cop slap jacked him again. Well, even while handcuffed, Dad broke the cop's arm and glasses and the judge sentenced him to five to ten years.

My dad knew a guy who lived near Bunker Hill, Michigan who came around sometimes, and after Dad was in prison I heard the man ask my mom for a date, and she told him "No". When cherry-picking time came around, Mom was picking huckleberries near a cherry orchard that that man used to pick cherries in.

My mother was choked near the cherry orchard on a grassy knoll, and then tossed in a pond. You know how the state digs for gravel for county roads, and the dugout area fills in to make a small, deep pond; she was found in one of those. I know it was deep because after basic training I went home for a couple days, and then I went back to Michigan with a cousin. I told my cousin I wanted to know the depth. I swam out to about the middle, and then dove down. It was cold like ice. I went down probably fifteen feet or so before I touched bottom.

She was probably already dead when she had been thrown in there, but it still bothered me a lot because Mom was always deathly afraid of water. Whenever we were swimming in a creek, Dad would try and entice Mom out of the shallow water, but she wouldn't leave it; she was scared.

The funeral director for Mom's services was a Mr. Miller. I went to school with his daughter for both first and second grade. I was in school the day before the funeral, and I left and went to the funeral home; entered in the back door. I went to the room where Mom was laid out in a casket; she was in a blue dress with a white flowery collar. She liked blue. Her hands were folded in front.

I sat in a chair there and just stared at her; I could see bruises on her neck through the make-up. Then I sensed someone near me, and I looked back over my shoulder. Mr. Miller had seen me sitting there and had come quietly, on tip-toe, up behind me.

"Mr. Miller?" I asked.

"What?"

"Mr. Miller, how was she killed?"

Well, he talked all around it; you know how adults do when they don't want to tell the truth, I guess because they figure you can't handle it.

Finally I asked, "Was she choked?"

His face kind of froze up and he didn't say anything, so then I said, "What are those white marks on her neck? The make-up doesn't quite hide them. I can see five marks there that are like prints, a thumb and four fingers."

He never said yes or no, and initially I was mad, but as I got older I realized that he probably didn't want to hurt me, and he really just didn't know what to say.

At times her death still does bother me. And you know there are things that can trigger the memories. To this day, whenever I see a mother and young child together, I think of my mother. Of course, it bothered me a whole lot more right after it happened.

6. A Horse Named Frank

My dad got out of prison after several months and we left Michigan and moved back to Kentucky when I was about ten; I think that's how old I was. I do know I was in the 4th grade. Although I didn't particularly like leaving my friends, we were going to my Grandpa Noah Rudd's place, which was a farm, and I really liked animals. He did logging, had a lot of timber, and, also had oxen, mules, horses, cows, chickens, let's see, geese, ducks, and I think, yes, he had some guineas, too.

My Grandpa Noah had him a buckskin horse named Frank, and a bay horse named Dan. Now Grandpa had gotten Frank from Texas, and he had been a rodeo horse. He was used to giving everyone a hard time, and he didn't want anyone trying to put shoes on him. My dad was Grandpa Noah's oldest boy, and he knew how to shoe a horse. He would pull a horse's rear leg up, put it across his knee, file the hoof, and put the shoe on; now I'm a-telling you, he could do it. So he told his dad he was going to shoe Frank. Well, when Dad first tried, Frank lifted his rear legs and tried to kick the stars right out of heaven.

Dad had never failed at shoeing a horse, and he said that you had to break the horse, because, if you didn't, you would have to fight him every time, which was just too dangerous, and also, too time consuming.

So again he tried lifting Frank's leg, and again that old horse kicked and jerked and caught the inside of my dad's leg. So Dad took Frank into the barn and got a straight bit and tied a rope to the loop in it, then he threw that rope up and over the rafters. He pulled so that horse's head was up quite a bit, and then went behind and put the shoes on him. A couple more times of doing it that way, and he never had any more trouble shoeing Frank.

Dad could shoe any horse or mule around. Now there were some guys who would say that if you had a rough horse you needed to put it in stocks, tie it down, possibly put a nose twist on it, or maybe even sedate it. But Dad said that was no way to do it; just break the horse, and then do it right.

I still remember that old buckskin; he had a pretty whitish color mane and tail.

7. My Hard-working Example

When I look back, I can see my dad was strict on me, and my mom was easy. They both loved me, and wanted the best for me; they just went about it different ways. Now my dad taught me to be a good worker, not only by what he said, but also by example.

When I was younger, I liked to talk to my dad and my pap (grandfather), and also some of the other older people in the community. My dad only went as far as second grade in school, but he was smart, and full of common sense.

As far as him quitting school, when he was in second grade he told Pap he didn't want to go to school anymore. Pap told him he would get him a pony to ride to school, so dad agreed to try that and see if it helped change his mind. He got the pony, rode it for a few days, but still didn't want to continue in school, so his dad let him quit, but he told him he was going to have to work, to learn how to make a living. My dad said he would rather do that than go to school, so Pap let him quit.

He worked for a man named Lou Marrs who had a lot of land, and was, actually, quite wealthy. But you wouldn't have known that if you'd have seen him on a street corner; he had longer hair, an old gray hat, and greasy clothes. He had really big hands; with cracked skin that made them look rough as corncobs. His hands were always greasy as a mechanics, and I don't think they'd have come clean even if he'd used a lot of soap on them.

And he always chewed gum, funny like, chomping on it, I can see him now, and, anyway, I found out when I was older that he had some gland in his mouth that didn't work right, saliva glands, or something, and he didn't get moisture in his mouth like most other people do, and so his doctor told him to keep a-chewing on a stick of gum like that to keep his mouth wet.

Mr. Marrs trusted my dad and made him the foreman. He knew that whatever job he told my dad to do, it would get done, and done right. Why, some of Dad's kin worked with him, but Lou knew he wouldn't be showing favoritism, that he'd make sure everybody worked the way they were supposed to.

And another thing I remember about Lou Marrs. In one of the pastures there was a large water trough in one of the corners for the cows, and next to it was a pump for water, you know, one of those kinds where you had to pump the handle. Lou had always told everyone not to go inside the fence as the bull in there was quite dangerous. One day everyone was gone from the farm except Lou's mother, and she went out to the trough to look at it, I guess to fill it if it was empty. Well, his mother went in there and that old bull saw her and run her down and killed her, sure as I'm sitting here talking to you.

8. Your Husband Never Washes

Mr. Lou Marrs' wife, Gertrude, was my schoolteacher one year. We boys would play rough outside and get all muddy sometimes, and when we come in she would get all onto us to wash our hands. There was no running water in the schoolhouse, but there was a little closet with a sink in there with a hose running to it and she had it hooked up somehow so that we could wash. Actually, some days I'd carry water in a bucket for the contraption, I guess these days you would say that I was brown-nosing to see if I could catch a little break.

Well one day I gave her a hard time about washing hands and she got a little worked up. I was kind of careful in my answers back, although I did smart back a little, but, like I said, I was careful not to say anything bad, because she would take a glass of water and mix a little soap in it and make a feller drink it. I had done that more than once, and I didn't particularly like it.

That night Dad was sitting around the table with his brother-in-law Goff, and a couple other guys. Goff was really named Magoffin, after Magoffin County, but everyone called him Goff. He had some brothers, and they were all named after counties, too. Anyway, I told Dad about the teacher getting onto me about washing my hands earlier that day. Now I didn't know Dad was joking, because he hardly ever cracked a smile, but he told me, "Tell you what; tell her to make her husband wash his big, old dirty hands." Well, I thought he was serious.

The next day in school after playing, some of us boys didn't wash, and Miss Marrs got onto us kind of hot and heavy about it. Later, just before the bell rung, she called to me and my brother Lester, and my cousin, NH. "Melvin, Lester, NH; you boys bring your books and come up here. The rest of you children stay in your seats until I dismiss you."

I was the first one up there. "Yes, Ma'am?"

She started talking real calm like. "Now when you boys come in tomorrow, I don't want you to get in the mud and so dirty like you usually do."

"Miss Marrs," I started, "your husband never washes, and he's got big, old dirty hands."

Well she dropped her glasses down a little and she just glared at me over the top of them, and her eyeballs got real big. I guess I had really embarrassed her. Then she jumped up and looked into a drawer where she kept a hose rolled up, the kind you could siphon gas with. She took that hose out and smoked me real good with it, right there in front of the rest of the students. I mean I had kind of heavy clothes on, so it didn't hurt me too much, but it sure embarrassed me, especially since it was in front of two or three girls that I was kind of stuck on.

Later, when I got home, Dad was there with Goff and the other guys, and Dad said, "I guess you got along all right with Miss Marrs today?"

"Dad," I replied, "I told her what you said, except I didn't say it came from you, and she went wild; she smoked my rear-end out real good!"

Well Dad and all the others laughed and laughed and clapped their hands together, and by then I had it figured out. They knew all along what would happen.

9. Flora Sue Shepherd

Like I said, I was in the 4th grade when I came to Kentucky, but I had a couple friends who were in 5th grade. I had talked with them some about what they were learning in school, and it appeared to me that in their classes they were just doing things I had already done in Michigan, so I just went in with them. I was able to keep up with the work, so I just stayed there. I don't reckon a feller could get by with that these days, but they were a little more lenient then, at least at that school, with that teacher. If you could do the work, you could be with that grade.

In one of my classes, I sat behind this cute little girl named Flora Sue Shepherd. She was a nice girl from a nice family, and I was a boisterous kind of boy, so I didn't really expect her to pay much attention to me, but I guess I was no different than most schoolboys in that situation, I could fantasize. She had pretty hair with pigtails, and I spent a fair amount of time looking at the back of Flora Sue's head, at those pretty little pigtails, and daydreaming. Yeah, I guess I was a typical young schoolboy. And, oh God, I use to jerk on her pigtails; she was a quiet girl, and she would never tell on me, but one day the teacher caught me, and moved me. Now, of course, I was trying to make an impression on all the girls, but I still kept finding myself glancing over at Flora Sue sometimes.

She had a brother named Bill; he was a grade below me in school, but we became good friends. We didn't live too far apart so we ran the woods together, played on the farm, and did all the things young boys did in those days. When I think back on those times, I realize how much fun Bill and I were able to have with so little. I shouldn't say so little though, because like I said, we had a farm with all the animals, the barn to play hide and seek in, and I'm telling you, in those woods we pretended to be soldiers, and robbers, explorers, and about anything else you could think of.

10. Pop Guns, and Slingshots

Something I liked to do when in the woods was to find an elderberry branch of a certain size and length where I could take another sturdy stick and push the center out and blow water through it to make sure it was all clear, and then I had me a nice little pop gun. You could take a hickory stick and make notches at an angle, and I can't really tell you what I'd do, I could show you though, if I had the stuff. You'd need some thread which you could wrap with lard melted, and at the other end of the stick you would put on a little knob. You could hit it and it would pop. If you wadded a bit of paper from a Sears and Roebuck catalogue, you worked it into the cleared out center, and when you popped that knob, if that paper wad hit someone, they felt it.

James laughed. But, you had to be careful or you would get caught, and then you'd be the one feeling something. Now you could follow the same idea, and instead of a paper wad gun, have something that shot out a stream of water. If you held your hand just right when popping the gun, that stream of water would set a fellow on fire.

James laughed again. I knew how to make a good slingshot, too, and let me tell you, I was death with one. I could pick off a squirrel with one of those, and if I wanted to have even more success hunting, I'd use those little small metal bearings, you know, the kind that went into the wheel bearings for bicycles. But I didn't just kill a squirrel for the sake of killing it; no sir, squirrels made good eating, and we depended on them to have a meal with meat sometimes.

James looked down, and then back up. I got into my

share of trouble as a kid; I guess I was just a typical boy of those times, but, now I'm a-telling you, my grandpa was proud of me if I brought in some squirrels that could be fixed for dinner.

11. My Favorite — or Least-favorite — Job

Now when I was a little older, I started doing what turned out to be a job where I got the least money, worked the hardest I ever had, yet, for quite a while, liked it more than anything else I had ever done, logging timber. There were some big trees in the woods back then, virgin timber, yellow-poplar, we called them; I think they are also called tulip trees. My grandpa said he'd heard tell that in pioneer days in eastern Kentucky there were yellow-poplar trees almost 200 foot high. He said he himself had logged one close to 150-foot tall, and that there were a few times where a truck would pull out with just the logs from one tree on it.

Logs were big enough that I remember an old man from Royalton who wouldn't sell his timber because he wanted to use it to build on the property he owned. So he used his timber for personal buildings for his family; new houses, smoke-houses, barns, you know what they'd use it for. And my grandpa said that man was able to build one small house entirely from one tree that was just plain huge.

After I was in the Army, I got into it once with a boy from Detroit, Michigan. He called me a liar when I told him how big some of the trees were. James laughed. I doubt this guy could even milk a cow. He probably thought you'd have to pump the tail or something like that.

Well, like I said earlier, besides farming, my Grand-pa Noah was in the logging business. He is actually who I was working for. Now, Royalton didn't have a saw mill, but Salyersville had a large one, so we would have to haul the logs there. Sometimes we would split the logs where they fell to make them easier to load. We'd take an old-fashioned hand-held auger, drill into the heart of a log, and then in the drill-hole put in a half stick of dynamite with a short fuse. When it was lit, and then went off, that would split some of those logs like butter with a butter knife.

Poplars and several other kinds of trees have a grain that is pretty straight, and, if someone knows how to do it, they will split fairly easily. Elm trees we had to use an axe and hammer. The grain of an elm seemed to me like puzzle pieces; it wasn't straight.

When we were felling a tree we'd use a crosscut saw, and sometimes if it was not leaning the way we wanted it to, then we would have to use a wedge to drive it in the right direction. A couple times when crosscutting a log, one would get loose and roll on down the hill and then we'd have to take a pair of horses and get a block and tackle, hook up the teams, and pull that log back up on the hill and around to where we wanted it.

Now a greenhorn starting out logging would be put with someone who had been doing it a while.

"James," my dad said, "I'm going to put you with that old man over yonder."

"Dad," I replied, "he hardly looks like he can pick up a saw, say nothing about cutting a tree."

"Son, that old man will work you to death."

"Hunh," I snorted. "I doubt that."

"Old guys can kill you if you try to keep up with them," my dad replied. "They'll work you to death, I'm telling you."

That old man and I cut either 41 or 42 logs the first day; the other two guys working in the same area as us didn't cut near as many. But after some time on the job I got paired with someone who started taking advantage of me, I guess because I was young and strong. We'd start sawing, and I'm pulling hard maybe eleven cuts my way, and he's pulling maybe half that his way. I mean, he'd lay down on me.

"You know," I told him, "I think I'm doing about 2/3rds of the cutting here."

"So," he came back with, "You're young and strong."

Now the thing I really liked doing was driving a team of horses; as a matter of fact, I'd have stayed logging if I could have kept doing that. But then there was this older guy who decided he didn't want to crosscut anymore, and my dad said, "Melvin, let so and so, I forget his name, drive."

"I kind of like doing this, Dad; I'd like to keep driving as my job."

"Now, Melvin, I want you to let him drive the team."

Well I cut timber another day or two, and then I left and caught a Greyhound to Michigan. When I got back my dad said he wanted to talk with me.

"Where've you been, Melvin?"

"Went to Michigan."

"What for?"

"Thought I'd see if I could get someone up there to sign for me."

Dad looked at me funny. "Sign for what?"

"I'm wanting to join the Army."

"You're not old enough," he said.

"I know. That's why I need someone to sign for me. Will you?"

"No."

"Why not?"

"Like I just said, you're not old enough."

Despite my dad's opposition, I joined the Army in March, 1948. Like I said, I wasn't old enough, but I lied about my age, and, even more importantly, I knew the girl who was working at the recruiting station. She kind of liked me, and helped me with getting the paperwork processed without any questions.

12. Think Pigtails

I went to what was supposed to be thirteen weeks of basic training. I say supposed to be, because while I was there the Department of the Army cut basic back to eight weeks. When I finished, I came back home with a seven day delay between assignments, and in Royalton I ran into Bill Shepherd, Flora Sue's brother, and, of course, I asked him how he was doing.

"Pretty good. You?"

"Well, considering I'm in the Army now, I guess pretty good."

"Yeah, I heard about that. Hope it goes well for you."

"Thanks. And, how is your family doing?" I asked. My strongest interest was in Flora Sue, but I thought it best to ask about the whole family, and besides, I was pretty sure she would have been married by that time.

"They're all doing quite well." He went on to tell me that he and one of his sisters were going to college at the time, at Alice Lloyd in Pippa Passes.

He paused, and then a little grin spread across his face. "'Course, I think I know who you really want to know about."

I reddened just a little bit as I replied, "And who's that."

"Give you a hint. Think pigtails."

I grinned a little myself. Caught! "Okay, Flora Sue? What is she doing these days? Is she the one going to Alice Lloyd with you?"

"No, she's a student at Lees College."

"She's in Jackson? Who's she married to?"

"She's not."

I was quite surprised when he relayed that bit of information. I mean, this was back in the 50's, and it was quite common for a girl to marry right out of high school, or even before, and when a young woman went off to college, a lot of folks assumed she was only going to look for a husband.

I just pursed my lips and nodded with a little smile.

"Neither of my younger sisters are married yet. You want to come by the house for a while?"

"Let's go," I replied.

He laughed. "I thought you might want to see them again. Or," he added, "at least Flora Sue."

I asked James about his feelings at his initial meeting with Flora when he went back to the house with Bill.

James shrugged. "I was okay; I mean I knew the family."

Flora Sue and I went together for a time, and then

I had to go back to the Army to my new assignment at Fort Leonard Wood, Missouri.

13. SGT York, Expert Marksman

One incident really sticks out in my mind from training on the firing range. I know you're familiar with the name SGT Alvin York, one of the most highly decorated American soldiers in World War I. I believe he was from Tennessee. Well, anyway, he was on some kind of tour and came out to the firing range during a training day. Think about it, this was a man who was a hero in WW I, but tried to enlist again for WW II, but couldn't due to health issues. In 1941, there was even a movie made about him, *Sergeant York*, which earned more than any other movie that year. Anyway, he decided he wanted to fire at a target, and told the training NCO that he still wanted to see if he could hold his own with a rifle. Well, he was getting older, and part of his health issues had to do with his eyesight, and the training NCO wanted to make sure that this highly respected Medal of Honor recipient wasn't embarrassed.

Back in those days, there were men who were assigned to stay crouched behind the berms while targets were being shot at, then when the firing ceased, they would go to the front of the berm, look at the target, and then signal the accuracy of fire back to the training NCOs watching through field glass binoculars.

So before the men were sent out to get behind the berm, the training NCO took them aside and gave the following instructions, "Now boys, when he fires, you make sure it shows a bull's-eye each time."

I don't know for sure what the actual hits were, but I do know that the NCO kept telling SGT York, "Great shot, SGT; another bull's-eye!".

14. Orders for Japan

Overall after World War II, things seemed to be looking better in the world and so when my unit received orders for Japan, we were quite excited. One of the reasons I joined the Army was I wanted to see the world; Japan sounded good to me. Only a couple things bothered me; one was leaving Flora Sue as I was starting to think that we might be able to have a future together. The other thing might be kind of minor, but never having been around the ocean, the stories I heard about seasickness made me just a little bit queasy. I never did say anything about that to anyone though. On the plus side, boys who had been overseas told stories about the ceremonies that took place whenever a ship crossed over the International Date Line, and that sounded like it might be fun; you know, there are a lot of traditions associated with the crossing. You are entering into what is known as The Domain of the Golden Dragon. Depending on which sailors you talk to, you enter the domain when you cross the line sailing east, or, according to others, sailing west. Although I didn't know it at the time, I would eventually cross over it a total of four times, twice on my trips over to Asia, and twice on the trips back. I've got certificates for each of them, so I'd say I've got it covered either way.

They always had a line crossing ceremony, a celebration with guys dressed as mermaids and all that. The ceremonies that take place are just for fun now, but they used to be taken quite seriously. You never knew what mood Neptune, god of the sea, would be in. He might be angry sometimes; in a playful mood other times. If he was angry, he might bring storms that would toss ships and all the sailors on them onto rocky coastlines and cause them to be shipwrecked. And nobody knew which side he might show, so the sailors would do everything they could to stay on his good side. Long ago, the sailors would sacrifice goats and oxen, sometimes by throwing them into the sea, and with a little luck, they would get Neptune into a better mood to where he might be kinder, and maybe even protect them.

Now they told us that another reason for these ceremonies was, at least until a hundred years or so ago, they were used to see how new sailors did on their first sailing experience.

Rituals used to include beatings, some of them quite severe, along with other things harmful to the health of the sailors. Thank goodness we didn't have to do that stuff; by comparison, dressing as a mermaid was not so bad after all.

James and I talked about how in the book of Jonah in the Old Testament Jonah convinced the sailors to throw him overboard in order to appease his God because he, Jonah, was in disobedience, and trying to run away. We decide this was a very early recording of a "god-appeasement ceremony.".

15. Seasickness and Saltines

The first time I got seasick was on our second day out from Seattle. On the whole trip over, we ran into typhoons a couple times; they'd try to avoid them, but it was still rough. The water was so high that when the ship was on the top of one of the waves it would seem like you were on a hilltop, and it looked like there was a valley in between each wave. That ship would go from the top of a wave down into that valley and up onto the top of the next wave. Man, I'm a-telling you, I was feeling sick.

Well, I got acquainted with an old hand, a sailor from Louisville, Kentucky, and he told me a trick to avoid being seasick.

"The next time you're in the commissary," he said, "get you three to four boxes of saltines. When the seas get rough, take you some saltines, and eat those crackers and drink you some water. Then lie on your back on the deck and look up at the sky."

I took his advice and it worked.

That seasickness, now, it really bothered a lot of them guys. They couldn't feed everyone in the mess hall at one time, only about a third to half of us. So there would be a line waiting from the lower deck to the mess. Of course, boys'd be lined up on the stairs, and sometimes someone higher up would get sick and vomit on the guys below. That was an unpleasant situation.

16. Swimming Through a Jellyfish

One place I was stationed while in Japan was at Camp McGill; actually, a bunch of us were assigned there so we could learn Japanese. Camp McGill was named for a Medal of Honor recipient during WW II. His name was Troy McGill, and he came from Knoxville, Tennessee, I believe.

Anyway, some of us boys were out on the beach there and we saw jellyfish out in the water. Now, me, I was just an old country boy from the sticks, and there was this boy from New York who had been near water all his life. He knew I didn't know anything 'bout any old jellyfish and so he decided to trick me into swimming out to one. He told me they were harmless, and that when you got up to them you could swim right into them and they would part for you. Well, he was right about the parting, but he was wrong about them being harmless; they stung me and it hurt like hell!

I asked James how long it hurt and he replied, "Oh hell, three to four hours, I guess, but those first couple hours I felt like I was on fire!"

I asked James what I thought was the obvious question, "Did you get back at him?"

"Probably," he replied. "I can't remember. I do know I was madder than hell, and if I hadn't been hurting so bad, I would have knocked him out as soon as I got out of the water!".

17. Boxing and the Sweetwater Swatter

When I was a kid, my friends and I always were kind of boisterous, I guess you could say. We liked to roughhouse around a lot, and, I mean, when we wrassled, we wrassled for teeth. There wasn't any kind of fooling around. So when I was overseas, before the Korean War started, I decided to see if I could get on the boxing team. I made it, and started boxing in Japan in the spring of 1949.

My main trainer was Lew Jenkins, the world light-weight boxing champion in 1940. He was in the Army, too; fought in WW II, and, actually later, during the Korean War earned a Silver Star for saving the lives of several men who got stranded behind enemy lines.

His start is an interesting story. His real name was Verlin, and he was born and raised in Texas and picked cotton in his early years. He was also a rough fellow, and he got the nickname Sweetwater Swatter because he started fighting in an alley next to a pie shop in Sweetwater, where the winner would get a pie. Now, promoters of that time would find someone they had heard about being a good fighter, and look him up, and make him an offer that was usually, we'll pay you a little to fight, and if you win, the amount you get will be a little more.

Lewis said he was out in a field picking cotton one day when a big Cadillac limousine stopped on the road and two guys got out. Hell, James laughed, he said they were in suits and ties. Well, he heard these men asking other pickers if they knew Lew Jenkins; his co-workers pointed to him, and so he went to the two men.

"You Lew Jenkins?"

Lew was curious about why these two gangster-looking men in the Cadillac were asking about him, so he was a bit wary as he answered, "Yeah, that's me. What do you want to see me about?"

James in Japan

"Well," one of the men said, "we hear you're a good fighter."

"I'm pretty fair."

"You interested in boxing Friday night?"

"What do I have to do?" Lewis asked. "And, what does it pay?"

Well, James continued, Lew said they told him that if he won he'd get, best I can remember, he said it was going to be $5.00 if he won and less if he lost.

"And, we limit what you eat for a couple days before

the fight, but, if you win, we'll buy you all the steaks you can eat."

"All the steaks I can eat? Hell, for that and $5.00, I'll win."

James grinned as he told me Lew said he won. Lew Jenkins was my main trainer, he added, and later, his assistant trainer also worked with me.

18. Sometimes James, Sometimes Melvin

At home they knew me as Melvin. Of course, you know in the military when you sign for something you use your whole name, in my case, James Melvin Rudd. In Japan, when signing for your pay, if you got over the end line at all, they red-balled you; only give you $10 until the next payday. Well, I wrote big, and also had trouble making the "J". I got tired of being red-balled, so I started signing just Melvin Rudd. This went on for months, and then when I got over to Korea, they saw in my papers that my first name was James, and thought I was trying to pull off some kind of bullshit. I told them the whole story, and was able to get all my back pay. I can't remember how much it was, but it was for a long time.

I'd get a raise every time I got a little lift on that ladder, you know, a promotion. Of course, every time that happened I would go on a drinking, womanizing spree. The MP's would get me, and then I'd get busted. I was on a roller coaster; PFC yesterday, Private today, and then do it all over again. I never got in any trouble while in Korea; I was good in combat, but out of combat, well, that was a different story.

19. $64 Words that No One Understands

I studied the military manuals as hard as anybody, and I also think I knew them as well as anybody. But I also knew you would always run into situations not in the manuals that you had better be able to figure out on your own. I would say that to new recruits when I had to teach some classes to them.

Now I think Southern dialect is the easiest to understand in the American army 'cause it's a slow speech, and, you know, also, when the higher ranked officers got to teaching they would sometimes use words and terms the average enlisted man couldn't understand. We had a Lieutenant from New Jersey, and when teaching he'd, well, he'd use words that a grade school kid wouldn't have any idea of what he was talking about.

One day, when both the LT and I were teaching new recruits in an outdoors class, a full-bird Colonel with a chest full of ribbons drove behind the class in a Jeep. He stopped and listened to us both for some time. After one of the classes was over he called the Lieutenant and me aside and said, "Lieutenant, I need to talk to you about something."

"Yes, Sir," said the Lieutenant, "what is it?"

I wasn't sure what to do. He called us both over, but it was the Lieutenant he had addressed. But I didn't want to be out of line by saying anything, so I just stood there. A lot of things were going through my mind; one of them, that I was scared. I taught those classes at a rather simple level so that a 5th to 8th grade kid could understand. I braced myself for him chewing the Lieutenant out over letting me teach, but then was surprised at what I heard.

"Lieutenant," he said, "how about letting SGT Rudd teach the class? He talks to their level. That's the way I want my men taught. You see, Lieutenant, a lot of men don't understand your level, but they understand SGT Rudd."

Then he turned to me and said, "SGT Rudd, these are your new men. I want you to give them a week of training."

Now that made me feel good, but I never let it show in front of the Lieutenant, and to the Colonel's credit, he didn't embarrass the LT in front of the men, and to the Lieutenant's credit, he never showed any signs of resentment toward me. He and I had a good working relationship.

20. Yuichi Akatsu

Let me tell about something I saw with a couple buddies one time, one of the darnedest sights ever. We saw a bunch of Japanese soldiers getting off a train, and there was one guy who was wearing Japanese clothes and there was quite a celebration going on for him. We found out that he was a Private First Class in the Japanese army, his name was Yuichi Akatsu, and he had been in the jungles of the Philippines since WWII had ended, still thinking the war was going on. He was part of a group of four, and they had orders not to surrender. The Americans were making broadcasts and dropping leaflets saying the war was over, but the leader of the group said it was all a trick. Apparently this guy was just tired of it all, and so he escaped and lived for about six months more on his own in the jungle before he surrendered to Philippine forces.

And the thing I like the most about the whole story is that we actually got to see him. Of course, years later, in 1975, I read in the papers about the leader of the men, Hiroo Onoda, who was finally convinced to surrender after twenty-nine years of hiding and surviving in the jungle. When I read about that I had a flashback, I guess you could say, to that train station and seeing PFC Akatsu getting off the train and being welcomed home.

21. Japanese Wives of Americans

Something else some buddies and I saw at a train station another time wasn't quite as pleasant to remember; when some GI's were leaving their Japanese wives to return to the States.

Right after the war, American soldiers stationed in Japan were told that they needed to remember that the Japanese citizens were not a liberated people, but rather, a defeated enemy. They were told not to fraternize, and although they could legally marry a Japanese woman if they wanted to, it was discouraged, and due to the immigration laws the way they were at the time, if they did get married, the wives couldn't go back to the States with them until they went through a long process, which for some of them turned into years.

Well, even with the discouragement from the military, there were still quite a few American soldiers stationed in Japan who got married over there. Like I said, I was with some buddies at a train station one time when some GI's were boarding to leave to go back to the States. Their wives were there with them, crying, and carrying on, which was natural, but after the train pulled out, several of them waited for another train coming down the tracks, and committed suicide by throwing themselves in front of it. That was a horrible image that I don't think I'll ever be able to fully get out of my head. We found out later that this type of thing occurred occasionally. .

22. KMAG

On Sunday, June 25, 1950 communist North Korea started firing heavy artillery into South Korea. They wanted to have a surprise attack before the South could get organized.

They decided to do this at the beginning of the monsoon season, which made things a lot harder, especially since everyone was already caught off-guard. The South Koreans left Seoul and headed south. The communists took over the city less than a week after they started the attack because the South Korean Army panicked, and beat it for a city called Taejon. There was a lot of difficulty and confusion in attempts to cross bridges over the Han River and we were told that in the first week of action the South Korean army was reduced almost by half from combat losses and desertion, from just fewer than 100,000 to a little over 50,000.

In war you make jokes about a lot of stuff some people might not think funny. There were some ROK divisions, and a group of about 500 American advisors, if I remember the number correctly, that were trapped on the north side of the Han River. The Americans were part of a Korean Military Advisory Group, also known as KMAG. The North Korean army was a few hours away from closing in on the river, and the KMAG managed to escape in small boats that had been left behind by the retreating South Korean army. The men in the KMAG said that they were changing their abbreviation to mean *Kiss My Ass Goodbye*. Of course, at that time, my unit was still in Japan, and even though we knew the war was serious, and that we would probably soon be involved in fighting, we got a good laugh when we heard that story.

I was still in Japan, in Yokohama with a couple buddies, having a good time, and on the street we ran into a couple GI's who had smaller packs than we did.

"Hey," I asked one of them, "how come *your* packs are so small?"

"Just got in from Korea. We're headed home."

"Why's that?"

"North Korea is breaking loose. Our job is over. You guys will be over there soon," he said.

"Who were you with?"

"The Korean Military Advisory Group; we're called KMAG for short."

"So what's happening in Korea now? We've just heard a little bit."

"You fellows," he said, "won't be going home soon, mark my words."

"So how come you're going home?"

"Our job is done. We were advisors to the South Korean Army. KMAG; now it really *is* going to stand for kiss my ass goodbye."

Due to the news about Korea, we knew it was just a matter of time before we were going to war. One evening some buddies and I got a pass to go into Yokohama to a popular dance club, the Olympia Cabaret. Upstairs there was a Japanese guy who sang and was in a band. I can't remember his last name, but you said it something like Jimmygen. He didn't speak English real well, but we all liked him, and liked listening to him sing. At some point during the evening he let any of us take the microphone and sing; he liked to hear what he called our "Hillbilly songs."

We also danced with the girls that were there, and were able to get pictures with them as we drank a few beers and danced the night away. Korea was coming, we knew, and we didn't really want to spend a lot of time thinking about what it might hold in store for us.

23. The Roof's Edge "Cathouse Buddha"

Another night, with rumors swirling all around that we could be headed to Korea anytime, three buddies and I, which included one of my best buddies, Austin, decided we wanted to go to Yokosuka which was just a few miles from where we were at Camp McGill. There were cathouses there, and we wanted to visit one, if you know what I mean. But there were some problems; first, we knew we were not going to be able to get a pass, and second, the perimeter to the camp was surrounded by concertina wire, and, as you know, it has jagged little pieces out all around its coils that are razor sharp, and, third, there were guards regularly patrolling the perimeter. But, we knew a couple of the guards on duty that night, so we told them if they heard anything not to shoot without checking it out first because it would most likely be us.

So we waited until they made their rounds, passing by each other going in opposite directions, and then we came out of a small shower room we had been hiding in. We had brought some barbed wire cutters and some lye soap. I don't know if you know this, but if you rub lye soap on the wire and then on the cutter blades it deadens the sound of the click when the wire is cut. We cut our way through the concertina wire and then started down the road, actually, more like a trail up and down the hills and through the rice paddies the seven to eight miles to Yokosuka. Overall it was pretty clear going and we also had no encounters with the military police, which, of course, was a good thing.

When we got to town we saw a boy and told him we'd give him a dollar if he would let us know a good place to go. You've got to remember that after World War II most of the Japanese had nothing, so an American dollar was a lot of money. He pointed out a house that had a large Buddha figure on the edge of the roof and told us we could find what we were looking for there. We told him that included in services for his dollar payment was that he had to keep an eye out for the military police and warn us if he saw any.

Well when we got to the place we paid in advance for what we wanted, were taken to a room near the back of the house, given kimonos, and told that we had to wear them. So off came shirts, pants, socks, everything, and we were sitting around on the floor the way the Japanese did, drinking a bowl of Saki, you know, rice beer, and wearing nothing but a kimono and what God gave us at birth.

After a few minutes the little boy came bursting into the room hollering, "MP comes! MP comes! MP comes!"

We were scrambling to get back into our clothes when the military police came into the room; it was just a little embarrassing, you know. Then one of the MP's asked, "Hey, where's the other guy?", and we realized Austin had managed to escape before the military police came in.

"Don't know what you're talking about," I said. "There's just three of us."

"Oh, I think there's another one," one of the MP's retorted, "but we'll worry about that in a minute. Right now you guys come out to the jeep with us."

They at least let us get our clothes on, and then we went with them. At the jeep they asked again where the other guy was, and again we denied there was anyone. Truth is, I knew there was another one, Austin, but I had no idea where he had gotten off to. There was a spotlight mounted on the back of the jeep and they went ahead and turned it on. They rotated the light so it was shining on the house, then started at the bottom and swept the light back and forth, going up a few feet to a new level each time.

They got up to the level where the Buddha was, and right next to it was Austin, sitting with his left leg against the figure, his right leg down against the side of the house trying to keep from slipping, holding on to his bowl of Saki, his kimono still on, and open, and all his glory hanging out, if you catch my drift. One of the MP's hollered, "There he is!" and about that time Austin's left foot slid, his bowl of Saki fell to the ground, then his whole body slipped downwards, and there he was holding on to the edge of the roof trying not to fall. It was a sight to see, trust me.

The people in the house had a crude ladder so the MP's managed to get him down, and then one accompanied him back into the house to reclaim his clothes where he had dropped them before scrambling out a window on to the roof, and let him get dressed. Then, believe it or not, the MP's just took us all back to Camp McGill and told us not to try doing that again.

24. Austin, Beer, Footlocker, and the Stockade

Let me tell you a little bit more about Austin. He had met up with a Japanese woman that he married under Japanese law, but it was not legal in the United States. He referred to her as his Mama San. Also, he could make a piano talk; I mean, he played like nobody's business. And another thing I remember about him was his laugh. It was very loud and sounded like "Ah-who-who-who". Very distinctive. You would never, never mistake his laugh for anyone else's. And finally, he liked his beer.

Now beer was forbidden in the barracks, so of course Austin brought some in one time and hid it in the bottom of his footlocker. Then he put everything back in place the way it was supposed to be laid out, but that beer made everything a little higher than normal. It didn't look quite right and it got noticed during the next inspection.

"Soldier," the Platoon Leader asked, "what's wrong with that footlocker?"

"Don't know what you mean, Sir."

"It doesn't look right."

"It looks good to me, Sir."

"No, soldier," the Platoon Leader continued, "your items come a little higher than all your buddies do."

"Sir," Austin replied, "I don't see how that could be. It looks fine to me."

"Well, you'd better remove everything and then I can see for myself that everything is all right."

Of course the beer was found and Austin was court-martialed and sent to the stockade.

When it was clear we would be militarily involved in Korea, General MacArthur ordered that all American military prisoners in stockades in Japan be released for war duty. I say all, I think they might have had an exception for if someone was in for murder; I can't remember. These men were to be picked up by an armed guard and escorted back to their unit where they would continue to be monitored by armed guards until the unit left for Korea. They would be issued their gear and while on board the ship to Korea would be kept in the hold of the ship, no handcuffs, of course, in case there was any problem where a ship would sink. At least they would have a fighting chance to survive if that occurred. Once the ships arrived in Korea, then the former prisoners were to be assigned back to regular duty with their unit.

Like I mentioned, Austin was in the stockade, and the First Sergeant sent for me.

"SGT Rudd, I have an assignment for you."

Yes, First Sergeant."

"This may be a difficult one for you."

"I think I can handle it, First Sergeant."

"You are assigned as the armed guard to go get Austin from the stockade and escort him back here. Think you can handle it?"

"Yes, First Sergeant."

"Now I know he's your buddy, and I know you guys tried to cover for him when the MP's caught you all in that cathouse in Yokosuka. So I'm going to make this easy on you, help you not to give into any temptation to be lax with him. You know what I'm going to do for you, Rudd?"

"What's that, First Sergeant?"

"If he escapes, you will be charged with his crime and punished accordingly. Got that, Rudd?"

"Yes, First Sergeant."

So I took a train to where he was imprisoned and upon approaching the stockade was greeted by big iron gates. I told them I was an armed escort for one of the prisoners so I was admitted to the guardhouse bunker.

"Let's see your orders."

"Here they are."

"Okay. Everything looks fine, so you just wait right here while we get him." So I waited until a prison guard brought him out.

"SGT Rudd, I am releasing this man to your custody. Do you know what that means?"

"Yes, I do, Sergeant."

"Well, let me refresh what you have already been told by your First Sergeant. You are to keep him under your supervision at all times, and if he escapes you will be charged with his crime and punished accordingly. Do you understand?"

"Yes, Sergeant."

"Then get him out of here; he's your problem now.".

25. Stopover at Austin's Mama San

As we headed toward the train station, Austin spoke. "Melvin, remember a few weeks back when we went from McGill into Yokosuka?"

"Uh huh."

"Remember we told the perimeter guards to ignore us if they saw us trying to cut through the concertina?"

"Mm huh."

"Well, I want you to do the same."

"Sorry, Austin, that's not going to happen."

"Melvin," he said. "I am going to try to get away, so you just let it happen, okay?"

"No you won't; I'll shoot your ass."

"We're friends," he replied incredulously. "You won't do that."

"These are my orders", I replied. "I'm not going to be put behind bars for you." He got real quiet for a while after that.

When we got to the station, Austin said, "Rudd, I need to use the bathroom."

"Okay," I said. "But leave the door open."

"Rudd! You can't do your buddy like this!"

"Told you I ain't getting locked up because of you."

So he took care of his business, but he wasn't real happy about it. Then we got on the train and started the rail journey back to Camp McGill. At one point we were nearing one of our favorite places where we had gone drinking in the past.

"Hey, Rudd. Let's go get a beer," Austin suggested.

Now Japanese rice beer was a lot stronger than American beer, about 16 — 18% alcohol, and I really liked it, so

I answered, "Austin, you know, I'd love to, but to be honest, I'm afraid to."

"Come on. Remember why I'm being released. We're going to Korea. This may be our last chance to have a beer."

"Okay," I relented, "but I'm watching you like a hawk." So we got off the train, I took off his handcuffs, and then we went into one of our old hangouts.

"Rudd, my Mama San is upstairs."

"So …?"

"She's got some beer."

"I'd like to, but I told you, I'm afraid."

"Look, you're being good to me by stopping here. I promise you I won't try to escape."

So we went upstairs and down a hallway to a little room and Austin went in to see his Mama San. I sat down in the hallway and put my back against the wall. I so wanted a beer, but I was also so afraid I'd get into trouble.

When we finally left I told Austin I was going to have to put the handcuffs back on until we arrived back at Camp McGill. Once we got back I turned him over to the First Sergeant who relieved me from my guard duty and assigned someone else to watch over him.

26. Let's Go Together

Delmar Cleaver was also one of my best buddies; he was from Columbus, Ohio, and we used to be on a boxing team together. We had been together by this time for at least a year and a half.

General MacArthur announced that battalions of the 24th and 25th Infantry Divisions, and the First Cavalry Division were going to be reinforced, and that the first 500 men were coming from Camp McGill. At that time, the 12th Cavalry was basically names-on-rosters only; they were mixed in with us.

Well again, even though there had been no official statements, we weren't stupid; we knew we were soon going to Korea. Then it was broadcast over the loudspeakers that anyone who wanted to volunteer for the 24th Infantry Division should report to the Orderly Room. Cleaver and I and one of my cousins, Marvin Rudd, decided we wanted to go to the 24th, so we went down to the Orderly Room to sign up.

"Since we're going to wind up in Korea anyway," Cleaver said, "we might as well be in control of our situation as much as possible, and decide who we want to be with."

Marvin nodded his head as I answered, "For sure, and we can look out for each other."

"Let's make sure," Marvin added, "that we get right together in line so we don't get put in different units."

"For sure," I answered.

We got in line; Marvin was 17th, Cleaver was 18th, and I was 19th. Wouldn't you know they cut off the men going to the 24th Infantry after Cleaver. I tried to let the officers in charge to let me go with my buddies, but the Army being the Army, they wouldn't make any exceptions.

27. Amphibious Landing

I was with the 1st Cavalry, and sometime after North Korea attacked South Korea we were marched into a large gymnasium and told we would be involved in a beach landing in Korea, the first such operation since the end of WW II. I'll have to admit, I was a bit scared, but also ready to do what needed to be done. Trust me; there was a lot of talk amongst the boys that night in the barracks.

When we shipped out for Korea, we put all our personal belongings into trunks and the Army shipped them home for us. There weren't nearly enough ships ready for a large troop movement and some boys had to go in Japanese fishing boats, but my unit was lucky enough to go over on the USS Oglethorpe. I've never been a cow in a cattle truck, but I have a fair idea of what it must be like. Just like on the ship from Seattle to Japan, we had to eat in shifts, and a bunch of us slept right up on the deck, where it also didn't exactly smell the best.

They told us that right when the North Koreans started their push south at the beginning of the war, they sent a steamer with six hundred soldiers on board with the mission of taking Pusan to make sure it could be used as a port of entry for our troops and supplies.

A South Korean Navy patrol boat discovered, fought with, and sank a North Korean steamer. Everyone on board died, but, more importantly, the port at Pusan was able to remain open. If the North Koreans had been successful in their attempt, the fight for South Korea would have been over on the first day.

And also, our First Cavalry amphibious landing was at Pohang because the port at Pusan was tied up with stuff being brought in for the other divisions already in Korea.

We were also told the First Cavalry landing was one of the largest amphibian operations ever put together by that time; one of the quickest, too. It turned out that there weren't any North Koreans resisting us on land or from the sea, so our ship pretty much landed on dry ground at the southeast coast at a place called Pohang-dong, north of Pusan. Weather, of course, has its patterns, and we had a bad luck weather pattern when we arrived. The monsoons weren't as heavy as usual, and in direct sunlight the temperature got near 120 degrees at times.

I mentioned it didn't smell so good on the boat, well, my first impression of Korea was, it stunk, too. They fertilized the rice paddies with human, I guess you would say, waste, you know what I'm talking about, and it was hauled to the fields in carts pulled by oxen. We called them honey wagons.

Another smell that was everywhere was kimchee, a dish they made from cabbage. They said it was fermenting; most guys said it was just plain rotten. Myself, I didn't mind it too much. Besides, I discovered much later it was good for a hangover.

We were not involved in any tactical movement, or fighting for a day or two, and then we got orders to move north. At first we had no maps, and it was easy to get lost, but then the higher ups in command got a bunch of maps from a Japanese collection. It turned out they weren't much good; most of them were old and had obsolete information on them because the Koreans would not use the geographical names forced upon them.

We heard that in a news conference President Truman wouldn't refer to our involvement in Korea as a war, but instead chose to use the phrase "police action". What we discovered was you can get just as screwed up in a police action as you can in a war. The political ways of saying things can be aggravating sometimes. Some guys painted "Harry's Police" on the sides of their tanks.

Another problem was we were being asked to fight a war after our military had been down-sized after WWII, and we just weren't ready, didn't have enough equipment or ammunition or training.

The Eighth Army was on occupation duty in Japan after the war, and Major General Walker was the commander. During WWII, General George Patton called him a fighting son-of-a-bitch, but in Japan all his units were under-manned and under-equipped. The First Cavalry was one of those units. We heard there were less than twenty anti-tank artillery rounds in all of Japan, and we already knew most of our equipment was stuff left over from the war.

One of the problems early in the war was many of the North Koreans had fought for the Chinese and had a lot of experience, but South Koreans soldiers weren't well trained. Hell, they trained with wooden rifle replicas in some cases, and had little to no combat experience. Most of them were forced into the army at gunpoint and almost immediately sent out to fight with little in the way of clothing or other supplies. All this led to some of the South Korean units having high desertion rates.

American boys knew this, too, and it affected morale. Hell, it's hard to fight for someone who won't do their part. And, on top of that, there really wasn't a strong reason to fight in a lot of soldiers' minds. It wasn't like

World War II where there was a sense of payback over Pearl Harbor; it was a Korean Civil War. But we were told that if we didn't fight here, the Communists would take over the world.

28. Our First Man Wounded

Our first man wounded was from Dayton, OH; although I can't remember his name now. He hadn't been in our unit too long; he came in just before the war. Let me tell you what happened. We had no showers, and those roads were nothing but powdered dust. You could tell someone or something was coming a long time before you could see them.

There was a river to the North, and we were dusty, so we hauled off and got in the river and were washing, and, believe me it felt good. All of a sudden, there was a "boom" from artillery, you know how you can tell when it's going over, and behind us there was a valley with a deep lake back in there, and we heard it land in that lake.

Well, I was the gunner, so I jumped out of the water, grabbed my clothes and went back to my position. James paused and grinned. Yeah, you can include that I wasn't even clothed.

We had a good platoon, and could tell when mortars were zeroed on us just from the sound. So we decided to make what we thought was a strong move and went into one area where the roads were so narrow we couldn't even turn the jeep around.

"Hey, boys; we got us a problem."

"Can you back it out?"

"I don't think so."

Now that was a fix, but we figured out what to do. We had enough boys that we just got ahold of that old jeep and went and lifted it around with manpower.

We made it back to our organization, and then the company commander got someone who could read a Japanese map. Our interpreter had been wrong; we were encountering the 10th Mountain Division of the North Korean Army. So the engineers widened spots in the road so that we could turn around.

A while later we encountered two North Koreans at a roadblock. We had had an American man wounded, and the next thing you know, the North Koreans were stripped naked and taken into the bushes. When the American soldiers got back into the jeep, there were no North Koreans with them. But we knew that the North Koreans didn't take prisoners, or at least not keep them very long.

29. Pushing North

When we headed toward Waegwan we were moving along a road, which by our standards even back then was pretty primitive. I mean, most of our roads in eastern Kentucky were better than that one. Now mind you, I said most. We usually moved single file, keeping some distance between each other. Every now and again there were a few small trees along the edge, and we could see to our front, way off in the distance some pretty large mountains. Sometimes I wondered if we would ever reach them, but you know how it happens, we kept putting one foot in front of the other, and they slowly got closer, and larger.

"Hey, Rudd," one of my buddies, Bristow, called.

"Yeah?"

"What do you suppose is on the other side of those mountains?"

"More mountains, I'm guessing."

"Yeah, but what's in them?"

"What we came over here for, I reckon; North Koreans.

"Yeah, you're probably right."

Sometimes we had to get off the roads and cross over rice paddies and berms surrounding them, and other times we watched bomb strikes; bombs and napalm drops. That was all quite a sight to see, and we hoped it was all hitting the enemy so we'd have it a little easier. After those times then we'd be going past hillsides all scarred up, and sometimes passing a lot of destroyed and useless equipment; jeeps, trucks, and tanks. If we got in a firefight, then we would dive for ditches along the edges of the road, sometimes having to lie in water. I might have been more scared if I thought about it more, but sometimes you just had to react and do what you were trained to do.

Some of the roads took us through some towns emptied out because the people living in them had fled from the North Koreans. But we knew that was also going to make it more difficult, because when it came to the civilians, there was no way of telling the North from South.

Digging foxholes was tough because the ground was so hard. But even though the times were rough, we tried to make light when we could. People that have never been in war don't understand that. You try to find some humor or you go crazy.

"Hey, buddy," I said one time, "that hole doesn't quite look deep enough to protect your ass."

"Damn it, Corporal Rudd. I can't dig any deeper. Feels like I've hit rock."

"You're probably right about that. Well, dig it as deep as you can and hope there ain't no bullets whizzing through at ground level. Otherwise you're going to find yourself wearing two cracks."

"I'll be happy to get out of this place without a Purple Heart."

"Yeah, I know. You especially don't want to go home with one where friends ask to see your scar and you have to drop your pants and turn around."

"You're right about that. So, anyway, what are we doing tomorrow?"

"Not sure," I answered. "See all those mountains in the distance over there? All I know is we'll probably have to head down this hill to look for another one to fight for."

"Man, Corporal, I heard we're headed for Waegwan."

"Who'd you hear that from?"

"A North Korean soldier stopped by while I was eating supper and told me," he joked.

"Well, hell," I replied, laughing, "why didn't you mention to begin with that you got it straight from the top. Next time one of those bastards stops by, make sure you shoot him.".

30. Have You Met My Friend?

I was sitting with James in his room when a nurse brought in his medicine and commented on my Stetson Cavalry hat.

"He's wearing spurs, too," James told her.

"Oh, really?" the nurse laughed.

"Oh, yeah," James said. "He just rode in here from Kansas. He was wearing that Cavalry hat, and riding on an old horse that is just starved to death."

About that time another nurse came into James' room.

"Have you met my friend?" James asked.

"No, I don't believe I have," the nurse replied.

"Well," James said, "he's an old Cavalry man from Vietnam who just rode in here on a horse named Suzie. Now he's kind of hungry, so when we eat here in a little while, I'm counting on you to let him come with me down to the dining room."

The nurse laughed. "We can do that," she said. "We'll feed him real good.".

31. Austin, Trucks, and a Piano

As I mentioned earlier, once the former stockade prisoners arrived in Korea, they were put back on regular duty. Well, my good buddy Austin was assigned a job as a jeep driver hauling ammunition from Pusan back up to Waegwan.

"You know what I'd like?" he asked one day.

"A beer and a Mama San?" I replied.

"That, too," he said, "but I'd rather be driving a 3/4 ton truck than a jeep."

"Good luck with that."

"Yeah," he replied thoughtfully. "You know that the officers who have those Mules make their drivers guard them like their lives depend on it."

"I guess they do, in a way," I said.

"But I've got a plan."

"And what's that?" I asked.

"Well," he started, "I saw the 3/4 I want yesterday in Pusan. I got the numbers off of it, and was able to use them to find out what officer it's assigned to." Austin told me the officer's name, which I can't remember, but he used it when he was talking to the driver.

"So what's going to happen? You going to walk up to him and ask him to give it to you?"

"Not quite, but like I said, I've got a plan."

And he did. One evening on a trip to Pusan he saw it was parked at an Officers' Club with the driver waiting with it. Austin pulled into the lot.

"Hey you," Austin said to the driver. "I am supposed to pick up this truck to make a delivery with it."

"I don't think so," the driver said. "This truck is assigned to my commanding officer, and I'm not letting it go anywhere."

"That's fine," Austin said. "I'll just go inside and tell Captain 'So-and-so' that the assignment I have is very important."

So Austin went into the club, stayed inside a few minutes, and came back out. "Driver, Captain 'So-and-so' said for me to take charge of this 3/4 while you go in and get the orders."

"No, I don't think so. I'm not letting this Mule go anywhere."

"It will be a real shame if the Captain has to come out here to tell you himself. You know he's probably gonna be a bit upset over having to do that."

After a little more back and forth, Austin finally convinced the driver that he needed to go inside and talk to his CO. Of course the minute the driver went in the club, Austin took off with the truck. He knew with the war just starting, and with the amount of confusion going on that once he got out of the immediate area he would most likely be okay. There were several of us in the area when he arrived back at Waegwan, and he was not only driving that 3/4 ton truck, he also had a small piano lying in the back of it.

"Austin," I asked in disbelief, "where in the hell did you get that Mule, and how did you get that piano back there?" Austin told us what happened at the Officers' Club, and then he gave us some story about making a deal with the motor sergeant to trade it back for a jeep, now that he had what he really wanted, the piano.

"Besides," he added. "It's probably not really safe for me to go back to Pusan with it."

"So, what about the piano?" I asked. "How did you get that?"

"Well, I stopped by a little church I saw on the outskirts of Pusan; I figured they might have one. They did, and so I paid a Korean man a couple dollars to help me load it. Then I high-tailed it out of there!"

I shook my head. "Ain't you afraid, stealing from a church?"

"Naw. God knows I did it so I could bring a little music back to you boys."

"Well then," one of the other boys chipped in, "let us hear some 'Boogie Woogie'!"

And he did. Austin tore that song all to pieces as we all clapped and sang along.

Once I left out again with my Infantry unit I never saw or heard of Austin again. I don't know if he survived the war or not. Sometimes I think about him, though.

32. Sometimes I Talk Too Much

(Basil B. Clark)

I was visiting James again, and Cora, my wife, came with me. It was the first time she and James had met. When we came into his room, James asked, "So tell me, Basil, did you bring your daughter along with you today?" Of course, Cora enjoyed that.

A bit later he commented, "Now, Cora, you two seem to be a pretty good match, but listen, if you ever get divorced, keep me in mind. I can take care of you."

"Could you put that in writing?" Cora asked.

"You know, sometimes I talk too much," James said with a grin. "And I don't always think things through. Let me tell you about one of those times."

"A while after I got to Korea I decided to write letters to three girls I kind of had a liking for; felt a little sweet on them, you know what I mean. I wrote the same letter to all three and just changed the name in the greeting. Well they all three went to Lees College and it turns out they all knew each other, and actually compared letters. Flora Sue Shepherd was one of them."

James looked at me and asked, "Do you know what we used to mail our letters?"

"Not really," I answered.

There was a dental office in Waegwan, and the dentist kept a lot of yellow stock envelopes, and we would get some from him. The envelopes didn't have any seal to them, so we would take a piece of gum from the C-Rations, chew on it awhile until it got good and sticky, then use some of that to seal the envelope. Of course, we didn't have to pay for postage, just put APO on it, and at the bottom of each of my letters I would put RLHASM; Rush Like Hell, A Soldier's Mail.

33. Pusan, and then Taegu

We had been told we would be reinforcing the 24th Infantry Division and some of the ROK forces. The North Koreans wanted to push all forces resisting them into the sea, so we knew our mission was to come into contact with them, and stop them before they could overrun Pusan.

We heard what the enemy was like in July when six Americans were found shot in the back of the head with their hands tied behind their backs. I remember thinking to myself, I would hate to go out that way; if I die I want to be fighting to the damndest of my abilities.

A bit after the middle of July, General Walker was told he had to hold the area in and around Taejon, and when he got those orders he only had the 24th Division available to him, but he knew he would be able to move us in the First Cavalry into reinforcement positions in a couple days. He tried to hold the area with approximately 4,000 men, and about one third of them wound up either dead, wounded, or missing in action. That came on top of earlier losses into the thousands the 24th Division had suffered in the couple weeks prior to this battle.

I was with the 5th Regiment, and on July 19th we started toward Taegu. At Yongdong, the North Koreans had the 8th Cavalry blocked from behind, and on July 25th we went to help them out. F Company got into some real heavy contact, and when everything was over for that particular battle, the 5th Cavalry Regiment had over 250 casualties. Believe me, the realities of war were sinking in fast for us boys of the First Cavalry, actually for all the boys over there.

Let me tell you something else, along that Pusan Perimeter we realized the only thing we had behind us was the sea, so we couldn't withdraw. We were in a hell of a fix; either get killed by the North Korean Army, or drown like rats. If we hadn't been able to hold on there, the Korean War would have been over almost as soon as it started, and there are a lot of us boys who did make it home, that wouldn't have.

On July 29th the First Cav was sent further north, and our regiment was NW of Taegu. I didn't care much for that road running north-south; for a short ways on either side of the road it was generally flat, with irrigation ditches and rice paddies, but beyond them, mountains, good-sized mountains. The road was called the Bowling Alley.

The North Koreans had a lot of tanks, P-34's, and we didn't have much to answer them with. Bazookas weren't real plentiful, and that's what we really needed to be able to knock them out.

A few times we crossed streams too deep for our jeeps and we would have to build a makeshift bridge for them with rocks from around the area. When we made the crossing high enough then we'd lay logs across it, and the jeeps could make it over. Let me tell you, it was a lot of work, but it had to be done.

When it was hot and dry, sometimes trucks, jeeps, and tanks kicked up so much dust you could hardly breathe. And if we were near a tank burning, phew!

It was rough. There weren't any front lines to speak of until pretty much everyone had withdrawn to the Naktong River. But the area they put us in, the First Cavalry, covered 35 miles, and our positions were so far apart that we couldn't even see the next one over. Once we were able to establish positions we could see air strikes at times, and called in artillery whenever we could see the enemy off in the distance. We fired a lot of mortars, too.

In early August, the North Koreans crossed the Naktong River with tanks and small arms and they overran a lot of American forward positions. Most of our problems in trying to defend the Pusan Perimeter were due to what I mentioned earlier, the Army being downsized after WW II. I mean, they basically neglected all the armed forces for five years. The whole First Cavalry Division took a hard pounding during this time period, and we eventually had to pull away from positions in the Yongdong area and move back toward Kumchon.

All the refugees fleeing the area really complicated things, too. We heard of several cases of women who looked pregnant who were in fact hiding items that could be used against us. We heard of one woman hiding a small radio that she was able to use occasionally to tell the North Koreans where the Americans were positioned.

One of my buddies, Roy Manring, experienced this kind of situation in the worst possible way. Our platoon saw some refugees headed our way, and we knew to scan them from a distance with binoculars. Suddenly Manring raised his rifle and shot a young girl coming right toward us. When the bullet hit her there was an explosion.

"She was carrying a hand grenade, no pin!" Manring hollered. "I had no choice. It was her, or us! God forgive me, I had no choice!"

It was things like this that made us suspicious of just about everyone. I felt sorry for Roy that he had to make that decision, but I was glad he did what he had to do. At that time I remember hoping I would never be faced with that kind of choice, but I knew I would come to the same conclusion as him if I had to.

34. Lack of Trained Soldiers

We had some .30 caliber machine guns, but we had to get orders from battalion, sometimes even regimental headquarters to fire our machine guns, and then they told us how many rounds could be fired; we only had 200-250 rounds for some machine guns.

Before I was wounded my first time in Korea, I was with an 81mm mortar platoon. One of our forward observers got wounded, I can't remember if he died. We didn't have anyone with enough training to work the 81, so I was one of three men that got chosen and sent up as forward observers. I swear, every night we had as many behind us as we did in front.

What few replacements we got, let me tell you the

honest truth here, many of them were just flat out of shape. And some of these new guys coming in didn't understand there were two kinds of soldiers; the quick, and the dead.

Let me tell you about the first time we got some new men. A truck came by and dropped off three to four new guys for every platoon, to be stationed at a gun position; their weapons were wrapped to stay waterproof. If they had been fired upon while coming out, they would have been dead before they could get ready to fire back. I got three new boys, and let me tell you, I was leery of them.

They were scared to death, and they didn't know anything about weapons. I got mad. I thought they were maybe trying for a discharge, so I sat them down on some railroad tracks. "Damn," I said. "Why did the military send you over in this condition? Didn't you guys get any training?"

"Well, Corporal," one of them answered, "the truth is, the only training we got was on the ship coming over."

"Didn't you go to Basic? How long were you at camp?"

"Yeah, in Seattle."

"Well, what the hell did they teach you? Did they train you in weapons?"

"We were only there for about seven days getting…"

"Seven days of Basic?" I interrupted. "What kind of training can you get in seven days?"

"None," another boy answered. "All they did was give us our shots and our dental work and issue equipment."

When I realized they were telling the truth, I took the time to train them. I didn't know how I was going to cram basic training into one afternoon, but we were expecting an attack; we knew that the North Koreans could do a full sweep in any direction, so I put a boy in charge to further train them. We had to teach them how to take weapons apart; hell, they hadn't even gone to a rifle range. They had been telling the truth about their training, actually their lack of training. We worked with them the best we could, and that evening I put them where I needed them, on a machine gun.

I couldn't get to sleep that night; I was afraid to. I knew the North Koreans could attack around midnight, so about 9 p.m. I took one good mortar man with me and went to check on the location the new men had been assigned to.

When we got to their position, we didn't hear anything. I went to the first boy—asleep; his assistant—asleep; and then I went to the third man, the ammo bearer…

James paused and looked at me… "Asleep," I said.

James nodded, and affirmed—"Asleep." He shook his head and continued.

I spoke to them in a low voice and no one moved. I was so damned mad that if I didn't need them I'd shoot them, but I had no choice, we needed them. So I told the mortar man with me, "Take their machine gun and their personal weapons and set them aside about ten to fifteen yards." After he did that I kicked those guys with my boot and woke them up. I asked them where their weapons were, and, of course they didn't have them; they desperately stumbled around for about a half hour looking for them, and trying to explain what happened.

I swear we didn't have one company in the whole battalion that was full strength. Easy Company was the rifle company, Golf Company was a large rifle company; let's see, James paused and cocked his head sideways, remembering, Howe Company was heavy weapons—mines, machine guns, bazookas, mortars, gas masks, hand grenades, I think that was it.

We had Able, Baker, Charlie, Dog in the 1st Battalion. If Able was in trouble, Dog would help; they were right behind them, actually right there with them.

James started counting off, E — F — G — H, oh, yeah, Fox Company, he added.

35. Nightmares

I had a pretty good buddy, Trenon Purser; we started our friendship in Japan over mutual activities. He was a heavyweight boxer. Anyway, because we were in the same platoon, we frequently wound up being in the same foxhole. One morning he asked me about the quarry in Michigan where my mother was murdered. I looked at him in shock as I had never mentioned my mother's death to him. "What are you talking about?" I asked. "Where did you hear that?"

"Last night. You were talking and crying in your sleep."

"Really? And I said she was murdered at a quarry?"

"Her name was Ethel, and you were upset with a Mr. Miller because he wouldn't tell you what had happened. You were talking about her lying there in the casket."

"Why didn't you wake me up?" I asked.

"I was afraid to. Because you were so disturbed, I was afraid to."

"Afraid of what?"

"I was afraid that might bother you, too. I just didn't know what to do."

So I shared the story with Purser. I also told him I had a suspicion about who had killed my mother, and that when the war was over I had intentions of going back up to Michigan to see if I could track the man down.

36. Action, and then a Lull

I don't know what happened to a Silver Star that I was told that my buddy, Roy Manring, me, and some others were put in for. We had set up positions for the night and were a bit worried as we had seen signs of recent enemy activity. I tried to relax, but couldn't. Sure enough, as night settled in, we heard the whistle of a mortar. As we scrambled to return fire, mortars continued to land around us. Then the North Koreans opened on us with gunfire. A couple boys were injured and we patched them up as best we could, and then a mortar landed right next to one of the boys and he took the bulk of the shrapnel. We knew he was dead before we even got to him.

We held as long as we could, but were overrun and had to pull back down the hill to a more secure area. There were a couple more boys killed by that time, and we knew we couldn't carry, or even drag, them with us. One of the hardest damn things I've ever been a part of was when we had to leave them behind. The injured men were able to go with us, but we knew there was no way we could get those other boys and survive ourselves.

The next day, a few of us went back to retrieve our mortars, ammunition, and the boys that had been killed. There were eight of us, and again the North Koreans tried to overrun us, but we were able to hold our position this time and stayed and fired the rest of the day, and all through the night. Those mortar tubes got so hot we had to put rags over them to keep them from burning up.

Around the end of August things slowed down for a while, and we thought maybe the North Koreans were on the run. It turned out they were just getting their stuff together for another attack. The First Cavalry was at Tabu-dong, and the North pushed us back several miles, but then they ran out of fuel for their tanks and had to end their offensive.

37. The August 15th Pledge

We were assigned an area to try and stop the North Koreans from crossing the Naktong River north of Waegwan. Other units from the First Cavalry were given the same mission at Tuksong-dong and Yongp'o to the south. The Republic of Korean Army's 1st Division was right north of my unit, G Company, 5th Cavalry Regiment. We were holding Hill 303, which was somewhat like a squeezed circle about two miles long. I guess you could call it a funny shaped egg. It was a tall hill; there was a peak that was almost 1,000 feet in elevation, where you could see Waegwan to the south, and also look right over the river. They told us that Hill 303 needed to be held because then American forces could be in a "King of the Mountain" position as far as keeping control of the main railroad between Pusan and Seoul, plus the highway that crossed the Naktong River.

August 15th was an important date; it was the day that five years earlier had seen Korea liberated from Japan. So

Kim II Sung wanted the war to end by this date. He gave the following order to the North Korean soldiers:

"Our victory lies before our eyes. Young soldiers! You are fortunate in that you are able to participate in the battle for our final victory. Young soldiers, the capture of Taegu lies in the crossing of the Naktong River. The eyes of 30,000,000 people are fixed on the Naktong River crossing operation."

"Pledge of all fighting men: We pledge with our life, no matter what hardships and sacrifice lies before us, to bear it, and put forth our full effort to conclude the crossing of the Naktong River. Young men! Let us protect our glorious pride by completely annihilating the enemy!"

But it didn't play out the way Kim II Sung hoped for. According to North Korean prisoners, in attempts to cross the Naktong from August 12th through the 14th, the 10th Division had some units losing up to 50 percent of their troops, with a total of 2,500 casualties. August 13th the North Koreans were pushing troops hard because they wanted to control Pusan by their self-imposed August 15th deadline. That meant they would have taken over all of Korea, and the high command of the North Koreans didn't care how many thousands of their men they might lose in meeting this objective.

One thing that did assist the North Koreans was that on the Naktong River they had a couple of underwater bridges; they built bridges underwater that were hard to see from the air, and that made it fairly easy for them to cross pretty much unnoticed at night. They used oil drums and sandbags to make them. We were told they learned this from the Russians who had done the same thing in WWII. So, on August 14th they were able to get a large number of forces across one of the underwater bridges and launch an attack on Republic of Korea forces just to the north of where we were dug in, and around noon our unit started to receive small arms fire.

Like I said earlier, our unit had moved to Hill 303 as part of UN forces whose mission was to fight off North Korean forces that were intent on crossing over the Naktong and gaining control of the city of Taegu. Taegu was a fairly big city, and its name in Korean meant "large hill."

We had two machine gun companies on our left and right flank, and during the night of August 14th, they slipped on out and never told us anything about it.

38. Identification (Shibboleths)

James and I talked about how passwords were, and still are, used for identification.

This practice dates back a long time ago; one of the earliest recorded instances was with Jepthah, a commander in the Old Testament in the book of Judges, chapter 12. Jepthah and the men of Gilead were fighting against men of Ephraim, and Jepthah knew that they dropped the "H" in some of their words. So, in the particular circumstances being described, if someone was trying to pass through the lines, they were commanded by the men of Gilead to say "Shibboleth", which meant either "ear of corn" or "flowing stream." The men of Ephrain would say "Sibboleth" instead, and gave themselves away.

There have also been stories that, also in WWII, German soldiers used the way Russian Jews pronounced the word for corn, "kookoorooza" as a way to identify their ethnic upbringing.

In Korea, the American Army would sometimes change unit names to try and confuse the enemy. Also, there was careful thought given to the passwords and countersigns. They did this in WWII also; they sometimes used words with letters that the Germans pronounced differently, for instance, the Germans said "V" for "W." We did the same in Korea. The Japanese and Koreans usually used a "W" for "R", so, for example, with my name they would say "Wudd" instead of "Rudd."

I just said there was careful thought given to identification, but there were cases where just the name of the person approaching was used. In any case, it was important to keep passwords secure, but in every war, both sides do whatever they can to tap in to confidential information. I wonder how my life would have been different if this apparently had not happened with my unit.

39. The Capture

Tuesday morning, August 15th, I was close to getting off guard duty about 5:30 a.m. when I heard what sounded like a tank coming down the road from where the South Koreans had positions. The other guards and I woke up the rest of the platoon so they could be ready if something happened. Then we stayed on guard, watching. Daylight was just beginning to creep over the area, enough that we made out the outline of two tanks being followed by a lot of North Korean soldiers. After they passed our guard post position, they went maybe a couple of football fields distance to where we knew there was a culvert near a curve in the road. Our platoon leader wasn't real sure that we had the right weapons to handle the situation.

He radioed for some help, and then told us to get word out over our radios that we were getting help from Echo Company, along with about 60 South Koreans. They were supposed to identify themselves by the name of their platoon leader, Lt. Pak. Then he, Lt. Pak, according to typical military procedure, was supposed to advance and be recognized and then report to our platoon leader. Now I'm not sure if the North Koreans in the area had managed to tap into our lines of communication, or not, but they had to have somehow discovered something because about 55 to 60 of them started back down the road toward our position. When they got closer to us we could see some of them had on Russian uniforms.

Our Lieutenant sent a man out to our rear to check them out, and when he got close enough, he ordered the soldiers, "Advance and be recognized."

"Lt. Pak."

Now, our Lieutenant wasn't sure whether to shoot or not because, along with those dressed in Russian outfits, many other soldiers were dressed with South Korean markings on their shirts, helmets, and soft caps. He was wondering if perhaps in the early light of dawn we guards might have been mistaken in our identification. About that time, some of us boys opened fire on the North Koreans because they were about halfway up to us, and shot three or four of them. Then two or three of them commenced firing and wounded a couple of our guys, so Purser and I fired on them. Lt. hollered for us to stop; said they were South Korean, but as they got closer we could see they were North Korean soldiers.

"Stop firing!" the Lieutenant hollered out. "These are South Koreans! The next man who fires," he says, "is going to get a bullet in his head!"

"Damn it, Purser," I said, "These guys are North Korean! I don't give a damn what the Lieutenant says, I'm not being taken without a fight!"

I was in the foxhole with my ammo bearer. "Look," I told him, "see that ditch down there. Slip down into that, and when Pak gets close, shoot him in the stomach."

"Hey," our Lieutenant hollered again. "Rudd, stop that man from firing! These are friendlies!"

"What do we do?" Purser quickly asked. "The Lieutenant told us not to fire."

"Shoot, damn it. We've got to!"

We started firing again, but it was too late; they were right on top of our position, and they were firing back. Purser got hit in the shoulder and the bullet went through and, further down, came right on out again. I grabbed my first aid kit to try and help him, and while I was stopping the blood flow, there were some North Korean soldiers that came to the edge of the foxhole, aiming their weapons at us.

I knew it was useless at that time to try and fight back, but Purser, probably not thinking real clear because he'd just been shot, I guess he just froze up and didn't want to let go of his rifle. I knew they'd kill him if he didn't give it up, so I kept at it until I could wrest it out of his hands.

Then our Platoon Leader ordered the rest of our platoon to stand down, and most of them were captured without any more resistance.

40. The March

By that time, it was getting daylight and we could see fairly well, although through a constant drizzle of rain. Our captors lined us up in a column of twos and took us down to a bank left of a culvert. Then while pointing their rifles at us, they ordered us to hand over our steel pot helmets, boots, and jackets. Some guys that were wearing watches had them just ripped off their wrists. As many of the North Korean soldiers as could swapped their pants for a pair of GI ones. After that they took our boot strings, along with some W110 wire, and tied our hands behind our backs. The W110 was field wire used to hook up field telephones to the command post switchboard, and they used more of that to tie us together at about three foot intervals and march us further down the road away from Waegwan. Some of the men were complaining about and threatening the Lieutenant because they thought that the reason we got captured was because of how confused he seemed while we were being approached earlier.

It was hard to walk at times; there were some guys pretty weak and stumbling along, and the stronger ones had to help move them along. At one point, a boy slipped over the edge of the bluff we were walking along, and the North Korean guards started beating on him with a trench tool shovel until they killed him. So later, when SGT Ray Briley, a boy from Tennessee, slipped over the edge, there were enough of us tied together that we could quickly pull him back up, but for those of us closest to him it was rough on the wrists; I really thought for a while that my hands might be cut off from my arms.

It was confusing to try and keep track of our totals

because they kept bringing in some new boys captured, and occasionally killing some in the group. Almost all of us were constantly trying to loosen up the communication wires they had tied our hands with; one boy managed to get his hands totally untied, and the guards started hitting him with a shovel. After they killed him they kept hitting him until they cut his head off. That just made us more determined to get loose. Some other boys managed to get a lot of slack in the wires and when the guards discovered it, they beat them with rifles and shovels and then they took them away; there were about ten boys, I think. We heard gunfire and the guards came back alone. We knew what happened.

I got stir-crazy mad and hollered in English, "Untie me, you sons-of-bitches, and I'll bite your throats out!" I was so mad, that at that moment I didn't even care that they would probably kill me, but they didn't do anything.

They took six more, I believe it was, the next day. Same thing. I felt like a prisoner on death row with an unknown execution date, but like the others, I still was trying to loosen the cords. Those damn boot laces were so tight; my hands were swollen for days after.

The longer they marched us around on that hillside, the worse my feet got; they were cut to pieces, marching barefoot like that. And you didn't dare hold back, no matter how bad it hurt; you know wanting to live is a powerful motivator.

I had pants on, but with no shirt, my arm circulation was cut off from the wire; it felt like my wrists were being cut in two. My hands were numb for days afterwards, and it was months before I got full feeling back.

We got no water, and almost no food. I say almost

no food, because, in their minds I guess, they did give us a little something. They had us lined up, and starting at one end fed us two apples. Now that wasn't two apples apiece, but two apples to be shared by several of us boys. Going down the line they held out the apples so we could each get a bite. I was near the end of the line of the group I was sharing with, and got me a bite of the core. And hungry as we were, they would eat and drink water in front of us, and then they even went and poured water out on the ground, while all we could do was watch. It was hot and them doing that was about the cruelest thing they could do, short of the beatings.

Anyone having to relieve himself just had to go in his trousers. That made you feel like nothing. James shook his head as he continued. Using the toilet in your pants … I didn't think it could get much worse than that; little did I know. One of the guards was a boy who looked to be maybe thirteen or fourteen who was real tall and slim. He pulled up his shirt once and you could see he had been shot. He was mean as hell and it didn't bother him to torture anybody.

Since some of us boys could understand some Japanese, we started to put things together and figure out what they were saying. Their orders were to evacuate us out at eight that evening and take us back across the river near Kajon to a prisoner of war camp nearby where they said they were keeping about 5,000 Americans. While waiting around, they tried to get information from us, but we all pretended like we didn't understand what they were saying. When it got close to eight, instead of taking us across the river, they took us back in the direction we had initially come from where there were now more

North Korean soldiers, tanks, and anti-tank guns. At a culvert, we were taken up a road to the left, and then into a dried up streambed. I'm not sure why they didn't take us over to the POW camp like they had said, unless they were afraid they wouldn't be able to get away with the river crossing.

The morning of August 16th, our Platoon Leader was able to escape up the draw, and before he left he said he was going to try and get help and come back and rescue us. That was the last time I ever saw him; we found out later he was recaptured by the North Korean soldiers and executed. American troops found him tied to the front of a jeep, his body sprayed with bullets.

41. The Guard That Was …

A one point after our capture, the guards had us stop at the top of a hill, and made us all sit down, still tied up. Down over the edge of the hill I believe is where some high-ranking officers were staying.

Now the North Korean units had some intelligence officers mixed in with regular guards to make sure that the men in their units were loyal. Most of the spies incorporated into their units could speak English. I tended to watch all the soldiers closely, and decided that you didn't need to be an Einstein to figure this stuff out. We were sitting there with guards at each end of our line, and an officer came up from down over the edge of the hill and motioned for two of the guards to come with him. I thought maybe they were going to be able to have a smoke break or something.

Like I said earlier, when we were captured they stripped us of all our personal belongings, but somehow with Bristow, one of my buddies, they missed some cigarettes and a picture of his fiancé he had in his fatigue shirt pocket. Well, he leaned forward and the picture and cigarettes fell out, and, of course, being tied up, he couldn't retrieve them, but he wondered if maybe one of the remaining guards would. Bristow knew that I could speak seem Japanese, as did the Koreans. You see, the Japanese ruled Korea for years, a good share of the first half of the 20th Century, and during that time they outlawed teaching, or speaking, the Korean language. So, Bristow asked me if I could ask one of the guards to pick up his fiancé's picture and cigarettes and put them back into his shirt pocket, and also if the guard would put a cigarette into his mouth and light it for him so he could have a smoke.

I told Bristow I didn't know if I could speak enough Japanese to make him understand, but I would try, and before I could say anything we heard in English, "I'll pick up his picture and put a cigarette in his mouth." I turned in the direction of the voice and it was a North Korean guard. I was dumbfounded as I had never heard him speak in English before. He moved around to where Bristow was sitting tied up and put the picture and cigarettes back in his pocket, and put a cigarette in Bristow's mouth and lit it for him. A couple other guys asked Bristow if they could get a cigarette and the guard lit for them also.

I knew it was a dangerous thing this guard had just done; that he could get in big trouble for this. But even before this I could see that this guard was different than the others by the way he talked to and treated us. He didn't holler at us or knock us about or kick us like the other guards did. Because of this, and because of what he had just done, I couldn't believe that he was a true Communist.

Now I could see that he had a machine gun with a drum that held around 60 rounds of ammo and an ammo belt slung over his shoulder that had at least another 100 rounds of ammunition in it. So, because he seemed to be kind, I asked how he could kill Americans, and, again speaking English, he said he didn't.

"You've never shot an American?"

"No."

I shook my head a little as I asked, "How do you know?"

"Because," he responded, "when firing I always aim high so the bullets go over their heads."

"Why do you do that?"

"To save their lives."

I was trying to sort this all out in my head as I asked, "Why?" I wasn't complaining, just trying to understand.

"Because," he said, "I believe according to the Bible that I shouldn't kill."

"Bible?" I was a bit confused, and very curious. "Are you a Christian?"

"Yes."

"Why are you in the North Korean Army?"

And then he told me his story. He said he was from a village close to Pyong-yang, and was the first born of six children to Buddhist parents who were very poor, so poor in fact, that when his younger siblings were born and started to grow, his parents couldn't feed all of them. They wanted him to get an education, and they knew there was a school a couple days' journey away, run by American missionaries. If someone could not afford to pay tuition, they could enroll under a work study program, and he knew that was his pathway to learning.

So, he and his father walked, he said, two days and two nights to reach the school to see if the missionaries would teach him.

Now, I don't know if they really walked forty-eight hours straight, probably both days and up into the nights, but he did say two days and two nights. He said on arrival they saw the mission compound was a small place as the missionaries did not have a lot of money for buildings.

The missionaries said they could take him into the school if his parents would sign consent for him to be taught the Bible, and because he could not afford to pay he would be assigned chores of working in the garden, preparing food, or planting rice. His father was agreeable to those conditions and so the missionaries enrolled him, saying they could teach him though the 8th grade. After a time at the school, the guard said he converted to Christianity and that his Buddhist parents didn't mind because he was getting an education.

The guard paused a moment and then continued with a pained look on his face. When he was older and back home with his family, one day some North Korean soldiers came by their house, called the family outside, and then said that they wanted him to join the Army. He said he didn't want to.

"Why not?" he was asked.

"Because," he said, "I don't believe in Communism, I don't want to renounce my Christianity, and I don't want to kill Americans."

He said his parents added they didn't want him to join the Army either.

So, the soldiers lined the family up; father, mother, him as the eldest, and right on down in age sequence to the youngest sibling, a small, very young, girl.

So, the commander of the North Koreans lined up some of his men in a firing squad.

"Let me tell you what we are going to do," he said. "We will first kill this little girl, and then go on up the line killing each child until we get to you. We skip you and kill your mother. You and your father will bury the family, and then we kill him. You alone will bury your father, and then we will take you with us, and you will be in the North Korean Army."

The guard paused ever so briefly, and then continued. "My mother was terrified, and just sobbing her heart out, and I just felt so bad for her that I told the commander, 'I'll go.' But I told myself I would never change, and I haven't. The commander spared my family, and also told me they would watch me like a hawk."

James had a pained look as he continued. About that time, the two guards we thought were maybe on a smoke break reappeared; I think they had crept back to just under the edge of the hill to where they could listen to our conversation. They hollered at him for being kind to Americans, knocked the cigarettes out of the mouths of the men who were smoking, and then went back down the hill again. As soon as they were out of sight the Christian guard picked up the cigarettes from the ground, lit them again, and put them back into the mouths of the men who had been smoking.

The other two guards came right back and knocked the cigarettes away again, and then started to beat the Christian guard badly. Again, they were verbally abusing him in Korean, and by the way they spoke and looked, I think they were saying they had suspected him of being a Christian and that now they had just confirmed it.

Behind me over my right shoulder was on open area with some foxholes dug in it and beyond that some woods. The two guards, who were carrying 7.62 mm Type 50 sub-machine guns, took the Christian guard's gun and ammo and marched him across the open space and into the woods. We heard burp gunfire and then the two guards came back to our position. We never saw that Christian guard again.

After the guard was shot, well…his death really got to me. In our country, people disagree over religion, and, I remember hearing as a child about martyrs, but I guess I just thought those were stories from the past. But this man died for his belief in God, he stuck to his belief under the most difficult of circumstances. I've thought a lot about the danger he put himself in to live out his faith. I have always thought that if I could ever get back to Korea and could find out his name, I would like there to be a memorial for him right there on Hill 303.

You know it still bothers me that he died because of what I asked him to do. I told Bristow, don't get him in trouble. And then we talked about him being a Christian. Had I known I was going to get him killed…I…I got him killed…if I had only known.

42. The Reckoning

On August 16th, Cpl. Roy Day, who also spoke Japanese, overheard a North Korean lieutenant tell one of his men that if the American soldiers got too close they would kill all prisoners. Later that night we were marched up a different route to the top of Hill 303, overlooking the Naktong River. We stayed there maybe 45 minutes and were under pretty heavy artillery fire from the American forces. For some reason, I still don't know to this day, they pulled four or five guys from the group and started beating them with entrenching tools. They also attacked some of us watching; I got hit in the head with a burp gun.

I understood enough Japanese to know they decided they couldn't get us across the river from that area either, so again we were lined up, marched back down the hill to a different draw branching out, and moved up into that gully. There were some places where it was hard scrambling, made even more difficult by having to do it with our hands tied behind our backs. We stayed there the rest of the night. The next day, the 17th, the guards lined us up to move us out again.

We were taken to another place on the mountain where there was some level ground to where they could plant rice; of course, during planting season they had water in the rice paddies. But this was the middle of August, and during July, August, and even into September it was so hot that the paddies were all dried up, making it real hard to get any water. In the spring, when there was water in the paddies, the source was snow melt from mountains.

Anyway, they took us to where there were bushes grown big along the sides and it was real hard to see much of anything to be oriented as to where we were. They lined us up on the berm, and then hollered for us to lie down, side by side in the ditches, tied together.

There were three guards most of the time, one at each end, one patrolling around the berm.

"Psst. Hey, Rudd."

"Yeah," I whispered in response. "What?"

"I'm dying of thirst."

"Me, too."

"What're we going to do?"

"I don't know if this will work, but when they're not watching, we could dig with our hands and try to loosen enough dirt to make a small pool of water. Maybe we can figure out a way to scoop some into our mouths."

"Shh. Guard coming back."

When the guard passed by us again he looked down with such a hard look on his face that I knew if we got caught doing anything he probably wouldn't care to kill us. On the one hand, there were images still freshly knocking about my mind of the Christian guard being walked across that field into the woods, and the sound of the burp gunfire. But on the other hand, damn, it was hot.

"He's further down now, let's try."

I don't know if you've ever tried to claw through dried out dirt in order to get some water, but when you're desperate as we were, that thirst will just about drive you crazy and you're willing to try anything.

On more than one occasion we would hear the guards hollering excitedly if they saw us, and then they would come and stomp on us and kick us with their boots. It should tell you how thirsty we were that when they went back to their spots, some of us chanced it and would try to dig again.

We could hear the sounds of American bombers in

the distance and felt a mixture of hope, and fear. Then the planes were strafing the area and artillery was dropping all around. All we could do was hunker down and hope the shrapnel flying all around would miss us. When the planes came, the guards ran off and hid, and we lay as low as possible. We could see bombs dropping all around; I can't even begin to describe the hell of all that. Some of them were hitting ravines nearby, so in the middle of fear that we could die any moment, I actually took comfort in knowing that they had to be killing some of the guards that had run into those areas. I remember thinking I hope they're getting those bastards, too.

There was a boy named Bragg, he was the third to my left, and when it looked like the bombs might hit us, he prayed, "God let one hit in the middle of us!"

I had a flashback to when I was younger and someone had hit a cement abutment that was over a creek and her car went over the abutment and into the creek; let me tell you something, something my dad said when she was in that wreck, pinned in the car and she couldn't get out.

"Oh, God!" she was praying, "Oh, God, please let me die!"

Dad busted the window to the car and shouted, "Don't pray like that!"

"Why not? Oh, God, please let me die!

My Dad said, "God won't take you if you are asking to be killed; you pray for him to save you."

And so I hollered, "Bragg, don't pray that way!"

"Rudd," he almost screamed back. "They're going to kill us anyway; I'd rather die from our own bombs than from the North Koreans!"

"Bragg," I hollered back, "don't think that way! You

can pray to God to save us, but not to kill us!" I wouldn't have said that to him, but I remembered my dad saying that.

And Bragg quit praying for God to kill us.

I believed what my father said then, and I still do now. We can't see or know everything that's going on in our life. God loves us, and wants the best for us. I do not see that He gives a man power to ask for something different than whatever He has planned for us.

Later I found out the bombing was done by dozens of B-29s and was the biggest air raid of the war to that point. And I think P-51 Mustang ground attack fighter bombers, re-designated F-51's by the time they were used in Korea, were also being used to attack the North Koreans who had captured us. The American forces knew we were on the hill, they were just not exactly sure where.

When the American planes finished bombing the area, I heard the guards saying there was an American company patrol below us trying to flush out and kill snipers, and I felt a surge of hope. But then some North Korean soldiers just over the berm called one of the guards over to them. They spoke with him briefly and he came back and spoke with the rest of the guards watching us. They lined us up like they were going to move us out, in small groups tied together. What we didn't know was the North Koreans thought they were going to get caught if they stayed there with us, so we were to be disposed of. About fifteen or so North Koreans came over the berm firing their weapons, and joined the other guards, all of them firing down into us.

Let me tell you the damndest thing that happened while we were being shot at. Maybe *damndest* thing isn't the right choice of words, but anyway, the minute the guards started firing at us a song I learned in church as a little boy came to mind and I started quietly singing it.

"Blessed Jesus hold my hand, Dear Lord. There is a Friend Who walks with me, To guide me day and night. Blessed Jesus walk with me."

James paused a moment, and then spoke again. "I thought we were all dead. I'm in my eighties now, but believe me, at that moment I never thought I'd see this moment, able to be here, talking to you."

I know the only reason I am alive today is because the two men tied to the right and left of me fell over on top of me. They were catty-cornered across me, and every time a bullet hit one of them I could feel them jerking, and I knew the moment each of them died. There was a change in the way the body laid across me. Blood from them was running down over me, but somehow, I knew not to try and wipe it away.

After the North Korean soldiers initially fired they must have thought they had everyone killed, and they started running up the hill to where there might be some cover and safety. Lying there, sure that each breath was going to be my last, all I could hear was moaning, hollering, and screaming. I guess that from trying to undo the cords earlier, there was enough slack that I could slip my hands loose, but I knew I wanted to lie there as if I was still tied. After a few minutes, the North Korean soldiers came back to check that they had killed us all. I had instinctively fought for survival by digging deeper under the bodies of my buddies already killed, and then lying real still. The returning soldiers worked from each end of the ditch they had us in; they would kick, and if you flinched they would fire point blank. This was all at men who still had their hands tied behind their backs. As they got closer to where I was, actually I think my training as a boxer may have helped me stay alive. My buddy Roy Manring told me later he was stuck with a bayonet while trying to burrow a little deeper under the man next to me.

As I said, I was lying with the two men on top of me…I can still feel when a bullet hit the head of the man with his head directly on mine…the bullet must have shattered in him according to what medics said later. That's when I wanted to wipe at the blood running across my head and over my left eye, but something told me not to move — after a while the soldiers who had returned quit firing into the group of us and headed back for places of cover and escape. I could hear the sound of them talking fading as they moved away from the area, and then it got quiet. I figured they were gone; I had been left for dead. I thought of my buddy Purser, and wondered if he was all right, and then I heard a voice, Purser asking me if I was okay. We soon discovered that we weren't alone; the next guy I heard speak was my buddy Manring, and I answered. Then a couple more responded, but we just laid there, not moving for about another half hour. The other four besides me that survived did so the same way, by burrowing deeper. All together there were five of us still alive. Six survived initially, but one died in the hospital the next day.

Then Corporal Day, Ryan, Roy, and another corporal out of G Company left the gully through a nearby apple orchard to get help while I stayed with Purser, who was very badly injured; remember he had already been wounded at the foxhole just before we were captured. I found a lid to a C-Ration can and used it to cut off my pant legs to bandage him. Shortly after the other boys left for help, I could see some troops coming across the hill, but at the time, I didn't know they were our troops. I figured when they got to us they would kill us, so I tried to get Purser out of there, but it was impossible; he was hurt too badly. So, I told him to lie there and pretend he was dead, and I would go for help as quickly as I could. I felt guilty leaving him, but I was also convinced there was no other choice.

I headed through the apple orchard also, but then heard the sound of someone walking through leaves. Since I knew there were North Korean snipers there, I laid down and drew myself up into the tightest knot I could and pretended I was dead. A North Korean soldier walked up behind me, and to this day I don't know why he didn't shoot me. I could hear the troops, which I later found out were the G Company patrol, and I guess he figured if he shot he would become a target himself. I didn't look up; I was waiting for him to roll me over to see if I was dead. The boxer in me took over, and I was thinking if he did start to roll me, I'd have a chance to knock him off balance and try to get away. By then I could hear the American troops quite clearly, and I heard the man behind me take off running, so I looked, and that's when I determined he was indeed North Korean.

I jumped up and hollered to the patrol that I was an American prisoner. They told me to come out to where they were so they could recognize me. I took them back to where I had left Purser, and we gave him some water, and then sent for medics who arrived within an hour.

James shuddered. You don't know how many times

over the years I've felt those bodies; sometimes when awake, sometimes they visit me while I'm sleeping. A good stiff drink helps subdue them, but I'll never be free of those moments until I'm dead and buried myself. I think the hardest part of the whole situation is knowing that your buddies, your fighting blood brothers, died around you and there wasn't anything you could do to help. That still drives me crazy sometimes.

But maybe that wasn't the hardest part. It was worse when CPL Day and I had to help identify the bodies, looking down at those boys that in Japan we used to go to town with to have a good time, their bodies now riddled with bullet holes...some we couldn't identify because they were so damaged...so swollen...skin turning black. I decided at that moment I was going to do everything in my power to pay back the North Koreans for what they did to my buddies. I barely knew one boy, another mortar gunner, a PFC I believe he was, Bruce Ream, but I do remember in Japan, the night before our unit was leaving out to make our amphibious landing in Korea, he was writing a letter to his fiancé back in the States, and he said he was telling her that he was going to be all right, to please wait for him. Damn it, he was one of the ones we had to identify. When I looked at the spot where I had been during the massacre, where the two boys had fallen, catty-cornered on top of me, their bodies formed a perfect cross. It gave me the chills.

You know, we used to go drinking in Japan, but that was buddies out having a good time. Ever since then, whenever I've had a drink it was to try and erase what happened. But some things get stuck in your mind; you can't erase them, that's all there is to it. I've tried to drown those memories lots of times when they appeared, but all I ended up doing was crying. Believe me, I've tried and tried to get rid of them.

James Rudd (left), Corporal Day (right).

43. Identifying Officers/a War Crime

Later, I was able to help identify two of the three North Koreans a patrol from G Company was able to capture. Their names were known from their identification tags.

When I identified the officer who ordered the killing of my buddies, I just flipped out, and several men had to hold me back. I would have killed that son-of-a-bitch had they not.

"This man, Pyong Tok Chon, fired an automatic weapon at our people lined up with their hands tied behind their backs. He was one of the soldiers who came up over the berm, and I saw Chon sometime before the shooting, going up and down the draw we had come up, checking something out, and then looking the prisoners over."

"And, this man, Kwong Taek Kim, and another officer who got away, were both carrying what appeared to be .45 calibers. I remember him from August 15th. He was with Chon when they came over the berm shooting, although I cannot actually say I saw *him* firing."

Details of the Hill 303 Massacre are outlined in the declassified report of a war crimes investigation dated Aug. 23, 1950. The investigation was conducted by Army Maj. Robert E. Brown of the Judge Advocate General Corps.

44. Last Rites

As I said, sometime after we were shot up, Manring and some others were able to crawl away. Now some of this other stuff I found out much later. Manring said his grandpa, who had been dead for four years already, appeared to him and told him he needed to hurry up and get out of there, so he did. After he got down Hill 303 he was discovered by American troops and received medical attention. When he told them about the massacre, Lieutenant Kelly, Platoon Leader of the Intelligence and Reconnaissance unit came with nine jeeps loaded with American soldiers. They had to travel through Waegwan which was emptied out and burning. Among them was Chaplain Kiner. When they got to Hill 303, of course they had to get out and climb the rest of the way. When they got to the site of the massacre, the chaplain performed last rites for the men who had been killed. These included my buddy SGT Bristow who had been hit more than 25 times.

45. The Hospital at Taegu

I was sent to the hospital set up in the former University of Taegu. I was in there three or four days. One morning right around daybreak, I was looking out my window watching Koreans lined up to shop at a fish market in the street below. And the damnedest thing, I saw men being pulled out of line, and right there being drafted into the South Korean Army. We heard they were sent into battle right away, no training, or anything. And in the early days they were fighting with no heavy weapons; they had M-1s, pistols, and hand grenades, that was about it.

I was hoping I would soon be able to return to the field. The officers in my unit did not want me to return to fighting because, they were afraid I might be recognized as a former POW and be singled out for execution, but I didn't want to let go of what had happened. I could just hear those bursts of gunfire over and over, the screams and moans, and the feel of my buddies on top of me jerking every time a bullet hit them, and I still wanted to fight in the area where I had lost all my friends; I was just overflowing with hatred and the desire for revenge. Eventually I kept on to my superiors until they let me back into the fight.

46. Back with the 5th Regiment

After I went back to my unit, we were still in the same general area between Waegwan and Taegu where it was almost a daily routine of "fight and drop back, fight and drop back". And, we were still so limited on ammo that we had to get permission for the 81's and machine guns, the bigger guns, to be fired.

On September 1st, the 5th Cavalry Regiment fought again at Hill 303 because the North Koreans had taken it back. We got to the top, but then were driven off again. It was hard to leave because I knew the blood of my brothers was still there crying out for me to do something.

September 5th, General Gay ordered the 1st Cavalry to move back to defensive positions, so once more we headed toward Waegwan which had now turned into a kind of no man's land. It was raining and it got so muddy we even had to leave a tank behind that got bogged down. We got to Hill 465 but couldn't get up it as it was too slippery, so we had to wait. Later that day it stopped raining and the sun came out, and it got hot as hell. We were told we would start an attack on the hill after dark.

We heard about an officer with the 1st Division who had been captured, his eyes poked out, a thumb jerked off, and then set on fire to die. When we heard about this we said we would never take a North Korean soldier as a prisoner of war, and if we did have one that was still alive, he'd best be ready, because he'd get messed up just like they liked to do. At this stage of the war, a lot of us were using revenge as our motivation to fight; I damn sure know I was. Bristow, Reams, and all the others were right there in my mind helping me lift one foot in front of the other, right there in my finger every time I pulled the trigger.

I had a buddy from Tacoma, his last name was Murphy, I can't remember his first. We had become good friends when we'd boxed together earlier in Japan; he was in the lightweight class. He had gone out on a patrol which didn't return when they were supposed to. We found the men later where a gully had washed down a mountain. A Sergeant had been shot behind both ears, and fell back into the gully. Murphy had tried to get the Sergeant back out of the ditch when he was killed, too. When we discovered him, he had both hands around the Sergeant's waist, still in position trying to help him up.

Something else that happened that I don't like to think about, but sometimes I can't help it. One time we were camped about halfway between Waegwan and a small village, I can't remember the name of it, and a little boy was headed toward us, and we could see he was carrying something small in his hands. Because these types of things, using children to carry out military actions against Americans, were becoming more common, I knew we had to take him out. And the fairly recent incident of Manring and the girl still stuck in my mind. We didn't have any choice. It bothers me, but I don't know what else we could have done.

Another thing that stirred up my bitterness and desire for revenge was an incident we were told happened in early September, I think the 3rd. Some North Korean guerilla soldiers came upon a radio relay station where they tied up and shot all the Americans there. They said the one doing all the shooting was a woman using a

Tommy gun. I think I could have counted it as just another battle but for the fact the men were tied up before they were shot. The night after hearing of the incident I don't think I slept at all as the images of Hill 303 came tumbling through my mind again and again.

On September 6th, our 5th Cavalry unit was told we had to withdraw from the Waegwan area. There was a lot of rain and mud and it slowed down everything. For a little while, on September 7th, Golf Company which had only about eighty men at this time, got cut off from the rest of the battalion. I remember the tightness that initially gripped my chest as I hoped and prayed we wouldn't find ourselves in a repeat of Hill 303. Around dawn we saw four North Korean soldiers coming toward our position. When we shot them, one of our sister units heard the gunfire, and that led to us getting reunited with them again. But I realized I didn't really want to leave as I could feel the presence of my buddies still calling out for me to get revenge for them.

We had moved to Hill 345, fighting there until a withdrawal a couple days later. We stayed engaged in back and forth fighting, gaining, and then losing from Hills 203 and 174. Hill 174 went back and forth between us and them several times in just a few days. There was one point where the North Koreans had one side of the hill, we had the other, and the battle was mainly conducted by tossing hand grenades. The 5th Cavalry lost so many men we weren't able to be very effective in combat, and on top of that, we were short on ammo again.

One boy in our platoon was an Indian; I guess the term now is Native American, but anyway, he'd come from the Navy, and he never talked. He'd get him a C-ration and just sit off to the side and quietly eat, and then clean his weapon.

The North Korean soldiers blew whistles as a signal for their men to start attacks. We got to one place where we were able to somewhat dig in foxholes, but there wasn't enough time to dig in places for our ammo. During the night, the North Koreans had managed to find areas to sneak men through our lines. My Indian buddy was dug in to my east but we were so far apart you couldn't even see the next foxhole over. It was early in the morning, foggy as all get out, with daylight just starting to break when I heard a whistle blow. I'd heard those whistles before, and a chill went down my spine more than usual, because I could tell that this time they were almost on top of us.

We got into battle and were lying prone out of our foxholes, but were so short on men we still couldn't cover our whole assigned area. I heard shots behind me and turned quickly to discover that my Indian comrade had killed four North Koreans who had managed to crawl through the open flank to our rear. Where the North Koreans had managed to break our lines, we were getting hit from both behind and from the front. We killed some, but they still about wiped out our whole platoon. As it turned out, one month to the day of the Hill 303 massacre, September 17th, I was shot three times in my legs and feet and this time was evacuated to the 49th Hospital in Japan.

I found out later that during the whole battle for the Pusan Perimeter, the 5th Cavalry lost almost 250 boys, and had over 750 wounded. The 7th Cavalry numbers were about the same. During that time, the whole 1st

Cavalry Division had a little over 700 men killed, and 500 of them came from the 5th and 7th Regiments.

47. Bob Hope

While I was in the 49th General Hospital in Tokyo, Japan, I saw Bob Hope and General Douglas A. McArthur when they came through on a morale-building tour visiting the troops. When we first heard they were visiting, many of us were either bed-ridden or in wheelchairs so we were wondering if we would be able to see them. But when the time came, we were pushed in our wheelchairs out around the stage, and the people in beds were carried out. We were all pretty excited.

Bob Hope, of course, had his troupe of good-looking girls with him, and there was one in particular, she talked to us, too, but I'm here to tell you, she was just beautiful and wearing a real tight-fitting outfit and the GI's just went nuts over her.

Bob Hope always carried a small baton. He flipped it when General McArthur came onstage, and asked him to sit down. General McArthur looked over at Bob Hope, and he never spoke as he sat down. Everyone was wondering what would happen next; we all got as close as we could.

"Some of you may know this fellow," Bob Hope said. Most of the people there tried not to laugh, but some did. "This fellow," Bob went on, "has got a cushy position." General McArthur never said anything; he just sat there and acted like he was real mad as he looked at Bob Hope.

As Bob Hope continued to make fun of him, I tried not to laugh. I about bit my tongue half off, but I couldn't help myself, and I soon joined in with some others, and we were all roaring before we got out of there. General McArthur looked at us as if he wanted to hang us or something. Seeing the general there acting like that, it raised morale, which was the plan, I guess.

"Of course," James grinned as he added, "having all those pretty girls around there lifted our morale, too.".

48. Decker from Texas

There was a boy from Texas named Decker I had been with in both Japan and Korea. He also had been friends with Delmar Cleaver whom I mentioned earlier. Now I told you how I missed going to the same unit as Delmar, but it turned out that Decker and Delmar did wind up together. Eventually Decker got wounded in Korea and wound up at the 49th Hospital in Japan the same time I did. There was a while the 49th was so busy and crowded that some of the boys had to be laid on cots in the hallways. Decker was one of those guys. Well, he found out about me being there and came to visit me in my room. I was really surprised to see him.

"Decker," I said in disbelief. "You're here, too?"

"Yeah, you know how it is; those North Koreans are just trying to keep this hospital in business."

"So, what's been going on in your life?"

"Not all good, that's for sure," he replied. "You hear what happened to Delmar?"

My heart skipped and my throat tightened because I

was pretty sure I knew what was coming next. "No, I haven't. Is he gone?"

"I'm not real sure what happened with him. He just went crazy in a battle one day and took off running toward the North Koreans just firing a .45 pistol, and cussing up a storm. They got him."

"Stuff happens in war that'll sure drive a man over the edge," I said. "Trust me, I know."

"Oh yeah," Decker replied. "That's for sure. Hurts like hell when you see some of your buddies wounded, or killed."

"Hardest damn thing I've ever done in my life," I said, "after Hill 303, having to identify guys we'd been with since Japan."

"Were you part of that? All we heard was a First Cav unit got captured, and about everyone wiped out while still tied together."

"Hands behind our backs. No chance to fight back. I was in the hospital for a few days, and then begged to go back to my unit. When Day and I were looking down at our boys, I swore I'd get those bastards back. Did my best, got a few, but then some of them got behind our lines one night and put a couple bullets in my feet. They told me I'm going back to the States sometime."

Decker gave a bit of a snort. "That's what they're saying for me, but I think I can outsmart these folks. Working on a plan with a couple of my buddies."

"Wish I could help you with whatever you're doing," I said, "but somehow this wheelchair limits my activities."

Decker and I talked some more and then a nurse came by and told him he had to go back to his cot; she said they had finally gotten him a room.

A few days later I saw him dressed in full combat uniform.

"What's going on?" I asked.

"If I tell you, you've got to promise not to say anything."

"I'm good," I said. "You can tell me."

"Me and 'So-and-so', I can't remember who Decker said, are going back to Korea."

"You have orders?"

"Nope."

"So how are you working this out?"

"Melvin," he said. "Think. When our units first went over, not everybody was able to go by troop ship. So how did the rest get there?"

"You going by fishing boat? Is that what your orders read?"

"Orders," he grinned. "Remember I said 'Nope'? Who said anything about orders?"

Decker and his friend did catch a fishing boat back to Korea. That was the last time I ever saw him. He was killed in action his second time back.

49. Birthday in Japan

My birthday is September 27th. Now the 49th General Hospital in Tokyo, Japan is not the ideal place to spend a birthday, but that's where I found myself the year I turned 19, in 1950. Now the hospital was really full, but there were two nurses there who really took a liking to me, and of course, I didn't complain about that. When I asked how long I would be there they told me they didn't know, but one of them asked me if there was anything I wanted special for my birthday. There was a club, KNO Tokyo, that I had been to from when I was earlier stationed in Japan, and I thought it would be really fun if I could get to go there again.

The nurses said they would need to get permission to do that, but they would check on it, and if granted, then they would take me to the club in my wheelchair. Well you know I was excited and spent some time anticipating the event; Melvin, I told myself, you may be in a wheelchair but it doesn't matter. For your birthday, you have got you two of the prettiest nurses in the hospital taking you to NKO Tokyo.

Two days later, they came by and said, "Sgt. Rudd, we are off duty tonight, and we are coming by later to pick you up and go out to NKO Tokyo!"

"I'm ready," I said, grinning from ear to ear. "I have got my uniform ready and my brass polished."

Well, you can imagine my disappointment when a half hour later they came back and apologized.

"We're sorry, Sgt. Rudd, but we can't take you out."

I was a little bit shocked and confused. Had I done something wrong? "Why not?" I asked.

"New orders just came down. You are part of over 800 men who are to board a ship and head back to Ft. Lewis, WA."

So, I was glad about being able to head back to the States, but I've always wondered, couldn't they have waited until the next day? I even asked if they could possibly send me back at a later time. Obviously, the Army didn't revolve around me.

50. Revisiting Michigan

I was in the hospital for some time in the States, and when I was released I had a couple weeks before I had to return to duty, so I decided to go up to Michigan to see Mr. Miller, the funeral director I mentioned earlier when my mother was buried.

"Mr. Miller," I asked, "Who killed my mother?"

"I don't know," he replied.

"I think I do," I said, "and if I ever find out for sure, and find him, I'll kill him as sure as I'm standing here."

I left the funeral home and walked across the street to the Sweet Shop where I used to buy candy and then decided I was going to get a pint of Old Dover, the same as what my father use to drink. A man named Paul owned the store, and he was at the cash register. There was a man there with his back to me who was buying some liquor and I thought I recognized the voice and I felt a prickly sensation on the back of my neck. While he was paying, I stepped to where I could see the side of his face. He glanced at me and got his stuff and took off. I stepped to where I could watch him through the window.

"Paul. Who was that?" I asked.

Well he hemmed and hawed all over the place and said he wasn't real sure. I pressed him some more, but he just put me off saying he didn't really know.

The man took off in his car. He was the one I thought, still think, killed my mother, so I decided to follow him. He had enough of a head start that I couldn't see him, and after about ten, twelve miles the road forked. Since I had no idea which way he went I just pulled off the side of the road to think about what to do. Two things struck me, the first one being that I had a 50-50 chance of going the wrong way and being in a futile pursuit. The other was that trying to get revenge might not be the best choice. I sure didn't want to wind up spending time locked up. It was with rather bitter regret I turned around and went back to town. I never did see him again. I did get some Old Dover and ran things over and over in my mind for a while. I decided I might be better off to try and let things go, and just get back to Kentucky where my next assignment awaited me at Camp Breckenridge, just outside of Morganfield.

51. Getting Short

At Camp Breckenridge I was about to get out of the Army and I made myself kind of obnoxious, well, maybe real obnoxious, about this. I would see new recruits and make fun of them because they still had so much time left.

"Say, how much time do you have left?"

"Just enlisted not too long ago; almost three years left!"

"Three years! That sounds like a lifetime to me! Of course, I have less than a week now, so I guess that's why."

I kept saying I was going to get me one of those red Corvettes they were just starting to build, and drive around with the prettiest girl in Magoffin County.

I guess you know I made some of those guys mad, but they wound up with an opportunity to see Karma at work. I had CQ duty at Headquarters, and I pulled it, actually not feeling too bad about it, because I was thinking it was my last one. I got off duty Sunday morning and started my

1/2 mile walk back to the barracks. Again, it was a rather pleasant walk because I knew I was leaving my last CQ duty behind me. My room was on second floor so I started up the stairs and when I was almost to the top, I could see a lot of my buddies sitting on their footlockers which had been moved and pulled up to make a semi-circle facing whoever came up the stairs and into the room. These guys were wearing their boxer shorts and T-shirts, sitting there with various drinks in their hands, ranging from coffee, to water to soda pop, and laughing and joking.

The closest guy to me as I rounded the top of the stairs was a tall guy from Texas who was sitting there with his legs crossed and a newspaper in his hand.

"Hey, Rudd!" he said loudly.

"What?"

He straightened his back, shifted his legs a little, and adjusted the newspaper he was holding. "When are you being discharged?"

Well, I poured it on. "I'm a short-timer, let's see, what is it now, three or four days; I can't quite recall. I do know this, though. You recruits can have all the days coming up; you can have this here Army. I'm through with it all!"

"Are you sure about that?" the Texas boy asked.

"I think I know my own discharge date," I snorted.

"I don't think you do. You have another year to go."

"I don't see how," I laughed. "I ain't reenlisted."

"Well," he laughed. "That ain't what I'm reading in this here newspaper."

"Newspaper?" There hadn't been a paper at the desk at headquarters where I had pulled CQ duty, so I asked to see the one he was holding.

"Oh, sure. You can read all about it in here. Three days,

Rudd? We don't think so!" All the guys started laughing and joking again, making fun of people who think they're short-time when they're really not.

I was getting a little mad, and real curious about what was going on so I said, "I'm going to take this paper to my room and read what it says for myself."

I tried to keep a swagger as I went to my room, and then closed the door and looked at the headlines. There it was in plain black and white; all RA (enlisted) servicemen and women were extended for a year, all US (drafted) personnel were extended for six months. Folks, I was madder than a wet hen. I threw that paper across the room and stormed out into the hall.

"Border, Conley, you boys ready to head to Evansville with me?"

Fortunately, Evansville didn't have the misfortune that Fort Wayne, Indiana had in 1910 when a vat in a brewery in the town collapsed while workmen were doing repairs on its foundation, and 18,000 gallons of beer spilled into the streets. Some of the men were in the path of the beer rushing out, and almost drowned before they were rescued. Although, not a bad way to go, I guess. I was in a mood, that if 18,000 gallons of beer spilled out into any street, you'd find me diving in for a swim, doing my best to help in the clean-up.

"Now?" Sgt.Border asked.

"Yeah, now!" I figured they would be ready to go as they were supposed to get out the same time as me. Border was a Sgt., I can't remember Conley's rank, whether he was PFC or CPL. I don't think he was a sergeant.

From Camp Breckinridge, you could cross the Green

River after going through Morganfield. We stopped about 1/3rd of the way to Evansville, at Henderson, Kentucky, if I remember correctly, to get something to eat. My throat was a bit sore, and my voice hoarse and I thought it might help it out if I had a bowl of chili with crackers and a beer. A few bites in and I felt that, if anything, my voice was getting worse.

I got mad and said to the waiter, "You got any of that red, hot, liquid pepper?"

"I got some that is hotter than a firecracker," he says.

"Give me some." When he brought it, I poured the whole bottle over my chili.

"Buddy," the waiter says, "that there stuff is going to burn you up!"

"I'm going to cure whatever's bothering me; burn it out of this throat."

Damned if that bowl of chili didn't set me on fire. I don't know if it helped me I not, I could hardly feel anything except the burning. So anyway, the boys and I went on to Evansville and got drunker than a skunk. Of course, under the Indiana ABC laws at the time, on Sundays, retailers were forced to sell beer warm, but on that day, I really didn't care. But as it turned out, there was something I did care about though.

This was still in the era when there was a lot of open discrimination took place. I don't know if it had to do with coming up poor, or not, but I was raised that all people were God's children. Now, I have to admit that I was still having trouble feeling that way about the people that had shot me up, and killed so many of my buddies, but back home in the States, it bothered me over the way some of my black fellow Americans were treated, especially knowing that so many of them had been right in the midst of the fight in Korea. So, anyway, a couple of black soldiers I knew came to the bar, and they were met at the door by someone working at the club and told they could get drinks, but they had to go around to the back door, and then they could only get drinks to go. Well, I went to the bartender and spoke my mind about the situation and we got into a heated argument. Some of his friends got involved, and then, of course, my buddies jumped into it, and we all wound up finishing our business outside in a back-alley brawl.

Someone called the cops, and when they arrived we got arrested and locked up for a while. They let us go early the next morning so we could get back to the Camp in time for reveille. I was worried for some time after we got back; I was afraid I'd get busted, but nothing was ever said.

52. Questioning My CIB

I decided if I had another year, I wanted to go back to Korea to see if I could get some more revenge. I still looked kind of young, and when we arrived they were assigning the outfits we would be going to, and I said I wanted to go to H Company, 5th Regiment, 1st Cavalry. Well, some Corporals and Sergeants noticed I had a Combat Infantryman Badge on my fatigues, and they thought I wasn't old enough to have already been over there.

"You'd better take that thing off, soldier."

"I don't think so; I earned this," I replied.

"If you know what's good for you, you'll take it off," one of the Corporals came back with.

"Hell," I retorted, "I earned this thing before you were out of basic training, probably."

Well they thought they'd sound rough and tried to force me to pull it off. I came back one more time with, "I earned this, and I'm not pulling it off for anybody. Check it out if you don't believe me."

So after they verified my status, they found out it was true and they didn't bother me any more about it. Then they asked all of us there if anyone had fought with the First Cavalry, and if we said yes, then again they checked our records. I don't know why they didn't see that when they were checking on my CIB. Anyway, they said I couldn't go back to the First Cavalry, I guess for the same reasons they didn't want me to go back to my unit after the massacre, so I was sent to the 25th Infantry Division, 14th Golden Dragons.

The 25th Infantry Division units were all regular except for one black battalion, and even that one had white officers; that's just the way they ran things back then. But they broke that unit up and made it mixed. None of the men in it had prior service with the 1st Cavalry.

53. The Wolfhounds

Our assignment was alongside the 27th Infantry, the Wolfhounds, and let me tell you, they were one hell of a unit. They aggravated us all night long, hollering, "Hey, Wolfhounds!" After dark, you could hear them from a long way off.

They weren't always that way. In 1950, when the war first started, Lt. Colonel John Michaelis, known as "Iron

Mike" took command of the unit. He discovered he had been put in charge of men that weren't even close to being combat soldiers. They were scared, in large part due to the fact they had little training for battle. Lt. Colonel Michaelis gave an interview to *The Saturday Evening Post*, and in it said, "In peacetime training we've gone for too damn much folderol. We've put too much stress on information and education and not enough stress on rifle marksmanship and scouting and patrolling and the organization of a defensive position. These kids of mine have all the guts in the world and I can count on them to fight. But when they started out, they couldn't shoot. They didn't know their weapons. They have not had enough training in plain, old fashioned musketry. They'd spent a lot of time listening to lectures on the difference between communism and Americanism and not enough time crawling on their bellies with live ammunition singing over them. They'd been nursed and coddled, told to drive safely, to buy War Bonds, to give to the Red Cross, to avoid VD, to write home to mother—when somebody ought to have been telling them how to clear a machine gun when it jams. The U.S. Army is so damn road bound that the soldiers have almost lost the use of their legs. Send out a patrol on a scouting mission and they load up a three-quarter-ton truck and start riding down the highway."

Now, like I said, they were one hell of a unit when I was fighting in the same area with them, but it took a lot of work, discipline, and battle experience for them to get that way.

54. Support from the Big Guns

During one monsoon rain, we were near a river where four tanks were crossing, men riding them, you know how boys would ride on the top. Well, we were back a ways behind them, and in the distance you could see water just rolling down that river. Three of those tanks got across, and then the water hit that fourth one, rising all the way to the turret. It killed the engine on that tank; fortunately, none of the boys were hurt, but later they said it was pretty scary.

It took me back in mind to a cloudburst when I was a boy, and we lived up a holler in Kentucky. Our house was along the bottom, and the creek overflowed and started up toward the house. I was kind of worried that the water might come up into the house, but it stopped just shy of it.

Seeing that water roll down that river in Korea took me back to Kentucky, it sure did.

Another thing I recall is one time we were on a hill and there was a Naval Officer and his radio man there with us giving support from the USS Missouri. The Officer would take the target grid coordinates and have the RTO call them back to the firing center on the Missouri.

I knew we were in aways inland, I mean we could see across a valley, and then there was a mountain range, and so I asked, "How're they going to throw them that far?"

The Officer said they could throw them over twenty miles. Then he pointed and said, "See that place right there? When I say, 'Fire!' you watch."

"What will I see?"

"Watch." A moment later he said, "Fire!"

At first I couldn't hear, and then in a few seconds a swooshing sound kept getting louder, then it went over us and I heard an explosion.

"Did you see it?" he asked.

"I heard it. I didn't see anything."

"When I say 'Fire!' pay close attention to where I point."

"Fire!" And then a split second later he pointed to a tree on top of a ridge, and I swear to you I saw that damn shell.

"What size are those guns, anyway?" I asked, and he said the shells were shot from, I think he said, 16 inch guns.

"They make one hell of an explosion," I said. "What does a shell weigh?"

"About a ton."

"They tell us to keep our gun barrels clean," I said. "How do you keep those monsters clean?"

"Large ramrods; real large ramrods."

I enjoyed talking to him, so we chatted a while longer, and I asked him about being assigned to our unit. "Oh," he laughed, "we were just floating around and thought we'd see if there was anyone who needed our help. We settled on you guys."

Now I knew that wasn't quite the truth, that they were ordered there, but still, he made it sound more personal. It also felt good knowing that somewhere in the commands above us someone knew we did need support, and then made it happen.

While we were in that area, we had a Lieutenant for a while who was a good fellow, but I swear he didn't know enough to get in out of the rain, if you know what I mean. He was the son of a multi-millionaire, and I figured he just never had to work for a living, or use common sense to try and figure things out. Like I said, I think he was a good man at heart, just not a good man to be in a leadership position.

55. Mortar Tubes/Piss Tubes

Let me tell you about a weapons inspection we had one time that didn't go so well. We were in an area where there was a Marine Division on the next hill over with a valley in between with some machine gunners that were all from Texas. We were kind of scrubby with our beards having six to seven days' growth, and our hair didn't look so good either. We were told that after we cleaned our weapons, and then ourselves, we could have a little R&R. So, we put up our tents, cleaned our weapons and put caps over the barrels, and then washed ourselves up. On the hillside, a screen was set up so we could sit and watch a movie, and then when it was over we went back to our sleeping area where settled down for the night in our sleeping bags.

The next morning, the Company Commander came to our area and we were ordered out for weapons inspection. I was 1st gunner for our mortar platoon and the 1st SGT ordered me to remove the barrel cap, which I did.

"Soldier, did you clean this weapon?"

"Yes, 1st SGT!"

"Yes, hell! You pissed in it! Who in the hell do you think you can kill with that mortar?"

Mine wasn't the only mortar that way; they had all been pissed in. We poured the golden liquid out and had to work for hours to get them cleaned back up. The Texans denied doing it, but we knew better. I was so damned mad at the time I could barely talk.

56. Ethiopian Misunderstanding

Once we relieved a Battalion of the 7th Infantry Division in the area of Pork Chop Hill after their well-documented battle. It was about the same height as Hill 303, and it got its name because they said that from the air, the top looked somewhat like a pork chop. The area we were in was near an outpost manned by some Ethiopians. We had to move up and it turned out they didn't understand the password, or countersign. They fired at us three times before we managed to get to a trench on the right side of where they were, figuring that we would try to get around to another outpost where we might be understood. I was leading my men, and I don't mind telling you, it was quite a harrowing experience. Besides it being dark, which was actually working in our favor, to our right we knew there was a bunker with gun positions, and trip wires laid out with flares attached. We made it, and successfully used the password and countersign at the next outpost, but it was close, let me tell you, it was close. Later on, some Marines moved into the area and we were reassigned to another mission.

And one thing I can say for the Army by this time; at least we had what you could call a decent Army. We were well equipped and had just about anything a fellow needed to fight a war.

Shortly after our assignment there, we got word the war was winding down and we were part of the fortunate ones to go back home. I was glad to be heading to the States, but still trapped in my mind were the many buddies I lost over there.

My new assignment back home was on my old stomping grounds, Fort Leonard Wood.

57. Marrying Flora Sue

It was after my second time in Korea that I asked Flora Sue to marry me.

When we decided to get married, I came back and we looked up a bailiff. There was a place, Howard's TV and Cable, and an old bailiff preacher man lived in an apartment there. I don't know what his name was; most folks just called him Mr. Bailiff. We knew him so we decided to go to him. Flora's dad was my best man. That was on September 16th, 1954.

I was embarrassed because at the time I only had $10 on me. I didn't care about the bailiff knowing that, but it bothered me that Flora's dad knew.

I asked, "Mr. Bailiff, how much do I owe you?"

"Son," he replied, "you can give me anything you want to."

Like I said, I was embarrassed because her dad was there, although, me being in the Army, he knew I wasn't rich, but still, here I was marrying his daughter, and he knew I had next to nothing in my pocket. I paid the bailiff five dollars; bought some White Lightening with the other five.

"White Lightning?" I asked. "What was Flora's reaction?"

"I don't guess that she cared," James replied. Actually, I don't think I told her. I bought me a half gallon. My $5 I had wasn't going to cover it, so I had me some clothes in a duffel bag, you know, pants, shirts and all, so I thought I could do some bartering. Well, unfortunately, the guy saw a field jacket he wanted. I wanted him to take something else, but he was set on that jacket. I finally gave it to him, and had to leave the $5 with him, too."

White Lightning was everywhere back then. Dad and his brothers used to be working up hollers a lot, and when, you know, they had to do their business, well, they didn't want to do it close to where they were working, so they'd go a ways down into some of those little gullies and all that were there, and there were lots of times they would find them a still.

Flora Sue didn't go back to Fort Leonard Wood with me at that time. She was able to teach with two years of college, so she taught and I went back alone. Later in our marriage, Kentucky passed a new law that teachers needed at least four years college to teach, so she went on to Morehead State University to finish her degree. .

58. Fort Leonard Wood, MO

I was still at Fort Leonard Wood, so after a while I told Flora Sue I wanted her to move out there with me, and she did. After she got there we lived on post for a bit, but then …

"Flora Sue, I have a question for you."

"And, what's that?"

"Do you remember what we were talking about last week?"

"James Melvin Rudd, we talked about a lot of things last week."

"I know, but think about the conversation about living on post."

"Have you found a place?"

"Maybe; I want you to take a look at it. Then it will be up to you."

So we went off-post and looked over the place. It was owned by an older lady.

"I know it's kind of small," the woman said to Flora, "but your husband said it didn't really matter as long as he could be living off-post with the woman he loved."

Flora Sue smiled. "That's what he said to me last week, too. Yes, it's small, but I believe we could make do in it."

And so we rented the place. Sure, it was small, but we didn't have a whole lot to begin with. We had happy times there. Actually, my whole adult life, when it came to where we were living, I was happy as long as I was with Flora Sue, the woman I loved. Oh, and, also, if we weren't starving; that makes you feel better, too. I've never been interested in being Mr. Money Man or anything like that. Just wanted enough to get what we needed, and to eat well. And starting there at Fort Leonard Wood, and then throughout the rest of my life, Flora Sue helped me a lot with taking one day at a time. Of course, I guess I'd done that while growing up, but she especially helped me with it after the war. "Don't worry; things will be okay," she used to say.

Now after Fort Leonard Wood, Flora Sue spent the

biggest part of her time teaching elementary school in Royalton at Salyersville Elementary School, although she did spend some time at a school at the head of Licking River, and one at Johnson Fork near Morgan County. She taught school for 31 years or so. .

59. Flora Sue and Nature

Flora Sue loved nature; I did, too. I wonder if her name had anything to do with that, flora has to do with plant life, you know. We couldn't be happier than when we had a little home someplace in the country woods with those timbers and creeks all around. We observed and learned from the animals, too. You know, up until recent years in the history of the world, people were mostly hunters and gatherers; that's what animals are, too. And animals can tell if a person is agitated or anxious; maybe we should pay more attention to that. When I was in Korea in enemy territory, I made it a point to learn the habits of the birds and animals native to that particular area. If you know how to read them, they'll tell you if another person, or even animal, is approaching.

So, when Flora Sue and I were out walking in the woods, I never worried about being lost; never have worried about that my whole life, I guess. I liked the woods when I was a boy, and then when I was in basic training, I took my classes seriously. I'd rather know how to read a compass than be able to carry ammunition. But later I realized I didn't really need a compass to find my way in the woods. I learned to study the direction of the flow of the creeks and streams, and I knew how to calculate direction from the Big Dipper and the North Star. And, of course, you can study moss growth on trees. I could tell you which side of a valley you were on just by studying that.

You know, I've dealt with some hard memories in my life, and you know I've tried to forget some of those things, but I do have to tell you that the times I felt the most peace in my life was when I was with Flora Sue. We were not party people. Flora loved raising things, and I think the times I felt best was if we were working in the garden together, or doing something with the animals. We were close together then. I tell you, if I could go back, I'd call it back, those times, I would. We worked hard, lived hard. We had no running water in the early days, got it from a well or a spring. We made and grew our own stuff. Made our own cider, ground our own meal, we'd kill off a hog and cure our own meat. Got milk from our cows and churned our own butter. I could tell time by the sun when I was out hunting, out shooting game for us to eat. We had a long creek below the house with the water as clear as crystal, and we'd makes us seines out of feed sacks, and could catch a good batch of fish.

I loved to go into the woods with Flora Sue. Now I knew names of some of the flowers and most of the trees, but she could tell you the name of every flower we ran across. She liked to get grapevines and then she would make wreaths of them. She used those possum grape-vines that grew wild, and, yes, she really loved to make those wreaths.

Flora started going to a little old church near the house, Royalton Baptist Church, and that's where she was saved and baptized.

60. Banjos and Other Things

When I was studying electronics at Mayo Technical College, we had to do a project for class, make something.

"Flora Sue," I said, "I have to come up with something for a class project."

"How many others are involved in it?"

"They're individual. Each student has to present his own thing. I've been thinking a little bit about making a banjo."

"You know, James, I think you could do that."

"I know I can if I just study on it a while. What I'm wondering is when I'm done if you could paint it for me? Not all over, but in some places where it would make it look better, you know what I mean."

"Sure. When you get it done, I'll see what I can do."

Well, I set about to design and then make that banjo. I had an aluminum handle on it, and used an aluminum pie plate for the head. I held a little car horn button, I don't know if you remember them or not, but I held one of them to play it. Flora painted the rest of the banjo a real pretty green, and where you tied off the strings, she put two white musical notes, just as nice as they could be. I got an A+ on that assignment. I also had to make a small radio for a project one time, and I got an A+ on that, too.

From the time of being small, I was always interested in how things worked, and that stayed with me. I was always fascinated with how signals could travel through the air and through amplifying equipment, and then how sound came out. The other boys in class got aggravated with me sometimes. The teacher would explain something to us, and then ask if we had any questions. I always did. The guys wanted out of class and I wanted answers. But I wanted to make sure I really knew something; I didn't want any half understanding.

A friend and I worked one time on making our own black and white TV. I still have the notebook where we wrote down all the diagrams and stuff. We had 370 separate pieces in that TV. I plugged it in and it worked well, except for one problem. The picture was good, but it was upside down. We had wired to the yoke the wrong way, had the vertical and horizontal reversed. When we changed those connections around, it worked fine.

Before I went to Mayo, I worked in Chelsea, Michigan at the Central Fibre Products Company. It was then that I decided to go to the technical college to learn radio and TV. I owned a shop three to four years, and had a pretty good business. I loved the work, but it didn't suit me so much dealing with some of what went along with it. I mean, there were some people, not all, or even most of them, but some, that would get their television or radio fixed, but when it came to paying they would hem and haw around, and try to get out of it. I hated that part of being in business for myself.

But I worked as an electrician all over West Virginia, Ohio, and Kentucky. I worked for Ashland Oil at the power plant in Louisa, and at a steel mill, too.

61. Pictures from the Past

I told you earlier about going to the Olympia Cabaret in Yokohama shortly before we left for Korea, where we danced with the girls that were there and got pictures with them as we drank a few beers and danced the night away. Well, again, we knew Korea was coming, and if we had known then what Korea did in fact have in store for us, we'd have probably stayed a lot longer, and made the MP's track us down.

And, if I remember right, I also told you how the Army shipped home our personal things. Well, Flora Sue got a hold of the pictures I had taken, especially one with some gals around, and us all drinking beer. She got kind of hot, and at one point after we were married confronted me about it.

"Who's this?"

"I don't really know."

"You don't know? You're right there with her, and you don't know?"

I shrugged.

"You were awfully close to someone that you didn't know."

"Flora Sue, we were just having one last night out before heading out to Korea."

"And you got some pictures taken that look like you were thinking about doing more than dancing."

I shrugged again.

Flora got even more upset. She asked a couple more times, "Who is she?"

"I told you, I don't know," I said. "It was just some girl that I danced with in the club that night."

Flora worried me to death for some time after about that girl.

62. My Children

My grandpa Noah had sixteen children, and close to one hundred grandchildren, and I guess sometimes a person reflects on all that. I know my dad did. The last time I saw him alive he told me, "Melvin, you know, out of all my kids, you're the only one I've raised that every one of his children graduated from high school, and all that wanted to went on to college."

He was right, and most did go on to college, and all but one graduated. But you know that didn't just happen. I used to tell them every so often, sometimes I'd sit them on the couch before the school bus ran, and I'd tell them, actually I was reminding them, "These are the things I expect from you that I never had a chance to do. I want you to finish high school, and then complete college." I'd usually add in, "I don't care if I have to pick up cans on the side of the road; I want you to get an education." And they did.

Now Flora Sue and I had eight children. First, let me tell you that all the children, within a year or two after they started school, were cleaning up after themselves and doing dishes. That was the one area where I thought Flora was a bit funny. She was very strict with the children in her classroom, but not quite the same way with our kids, so she objected sometimes, but I told her that the children had to learn how to take care of themselves. They all learned how to cook, clean, and they all worked in the garden and mowed grass, and I also used to tell them I didn't want to catch them sassing, or in other ways being disrespectful.

My oldest boy, William, was born while we were at

Ft. Leonard Wood, Missouri. As he grew, just like when I was his age, he liked to try and figure things out. When he was older, I can't remember exactly how old, there was a family nearby that raised tobacco and they had an old machine shop with a real old lathe in it that had a bad motor. The guy had a brother named Cecil who said he could fix it, but try as he could, he couldn't. Finally, he asked William to draw him a diagram and explain it. William kept at it, redrew the diagram five or six times, and then explained it all to Cecil, and they got it working.

William made a career out of the military; at one time he was an Army Blackhawk pilot during Operation Urgent Fury in Granada. He went to Germany several times, and he was also in Desert Storm with the 101st Airborne Division as an Aircraft Maintenance Officer. Let's see if I can remember all these, I believe he was also stationed at Ft. Campbell, Kentucky; Fairbanks, Alaska; and Ft. Lewis, Washington. He stayed near Ft Lewis when he got out because his wife's family was near there. William and his wife have two children and four grandchildren. Their oldest son, also named James, went to Iraq and Kuwait, too. I think he was in Military Intelligence.

Melissa was always a rather quiet and obedient child, and was always a good student. Like her mother, she loved to garden. I remember one incident with Melissa on a merry-go-round that was one of the scariest times I ever had, well, maybe after Hill 303. She was playing, and Flora Sue and I joined her, and I started pushing the merry-go-round real fast, and she was loving it. But then Melissa lost her hold and went flying off, hit her head, and was knocked out. She came to pretty soon after, but it put the scare into me, I'll tell you. She didn't want to go on that merry-go-round again for some time, but I told her I would make her manager of the see-saw, and she was happy with that.

Melissa attended four years of college at Morehead State University, and did an intern in Beckley, West Virginia. She earned a Bachelor degree in the medical technology field.

Malinda was always real quiet, kind of like her mother, and my father-in-law. James laughed. She was the opposite of me in that area. She attended Western Kentucky University where she earned a Bachelor of Science Degree with an area of concentration in Recreation. She has a real strong faith in God and is a wonderful mother and grandmother. She is also very good at making quilts. Malinda and her husband have five children and five grandchildren.

Now after high school, Ralph joined the Army, was with the 82nd Airborne Division, and he made a lot of jumps in his day. When there were problems going on around the world, his unit was often placed on alert, to respond within 18 hours if necessary to keep Americans safe. Like any father would be, I was pretty proud of that. He got out of service and started at Mayo State Vocational School in Paintsville, Kentucky, but after six months he said he wanted to talk to his mother and me.

"What is it, son?"

"Well, Dad, I'm just wasting your money going to school."

"What do you mean?"

"I just don't have any interest in my classes. I'd rather get a job."

"But, Ralph, you know what I've always expected from you."

Flora Sue jumped into the conversation. "Now, Melvin, he's old enough to decide for himself what he wants to do."

"You're not going to lay around the house," I said.

"I want to work, dad. I want to get out and get a job."

"Melvin," Flora Sue came back, "you can't force what a person is going to be interested in."

Well I knew she had a valid point, and I appreciated the fact that Ralph was being honest with us. I mean, he could have gone on in school for some time, maybe just having fun with his friends, and, as he put it, wasting our money. So, I consented to his dropping out, he got a job, and has done real well with his life. Ralph has always been an easy going kind of guy, although I guess I could tell you about the time he got upset with a teacher and went and let the air out of one of her tires. Trust me; he had to go apologize to the teacher.

Marla graduated from high school and headed to Bowling Green to attend Western Kentucky University. She only attended a semester and a half. Marla wanted to join the military, and to be honest, at first I wasn't for it. I guess you could say I was still a bit old-school, and especially with my own experiences in Korea, I just didn't think it best for a girl to be in the service. I knew many served with honor and distinction, but this was my daughter, and it kind of seemed too close to home, if you know what I mean. I guess, at least subconsciously, and probably consciously, too, I was afraid she might someday have to face something like what I went through, and I was afraid for her.

But she joined up; she told me to remember that she was right there when I used to tell the boys it was their patriotic duty to serve their country. "I'm going to do that, too," she said. She was in the Air Force and stationed at Lawson Army Airfield, I believe it was, at Ft. Benning, Georgia. She had something to do with Sheet Metal and structure repairs on the aircraft. She was later assigned to Pope AFB, North Carolina, the base that supports the 82nd Airborne Division with its Worldwide 'No Notice' deployment requirement, the base that American troops have shipped out from to Granada, Panama, the Middle East, anywhere Americans or American interests are threatened. Marla and her husband have three children and four grandchildren.

Michael, whenever he was home, always took over mowing the grass; he loved doing that. He also could be mischievous and would walk a mile to get a joke on you.

He studied radio and TV at Mayo Technical College and graduated top of his class. He was very inquisitive, and after the others were in bed, I would find him sometimes sitting on the floor drawing diagrams. He was always thinking about making a better radio, or how to come up with some way to have an automatic AC/DC radio in a car. I had a Buick that was on the receiving end of most of his experimentation.

He was in the National Guard based at Jackson, Kentucky, and taught some classes during training times there. If someone didn't understand the material he presented, he said he would just keep at it until they did.

He had a Thunderbird, I think it was, with a sliding

'T' top, and he always liked to drive fast; he would keep that pedal to the metal. Unfortunately, his fast driving caught up to him one day and he was killed in a car accident.

Lana was a determined young girl. I think I may have used the word stubborn with her a time or two, but I've come to believe determined is a better description. She attended college at Morehead State University and did real well, earning a Bachelor Degree in Social Work with a primary focus on health care. A medical social worker for 26 years, her jobs have included Hospice, Home Health, Nursing Home, and currently, a hospital social worker.

Stephen is the youngest boy. He was quiet, also more like his mother than me in that department. He didn't raise Cain, although he would occasionally prank a little. After high school, he joined the US Army. He was responsible for communications, and was stationed with a Multiple Launch Rocket System (MLRS) unit at Ft. Sill, Oklahoma when that system was fielded. He did a lot of training in Oklahoma and throughout the desert southwest.

After leaving active duty, he joined the National Guard Unit at Morehead. Stephen enrolled at Morehead State University and completed four years of college, earning a Bachelor Degree in Environmental Science. He works for the State as a supervisor for Environmental Services at the Health Department. His job duties include inspections for food service establishments and sanitation system installations. He is also interested in family histories and has done extensive genealogy research into our family tree. Stephen and his wife have two children.

Interestingly, Stephen and Lana enrolled at Morehead State University together; both completing four years of college, and graduated together in 1991.

63. Folks From the Past

Remember I told you earlier about the first man in our unit that was injured, the man from Dayton, OH. The next time I saw him was after the war, I was with my wife driving in Dayton in the 1947 maroon Ford I had recently bought. We were on a four-lane road, and stopped at a light. When it changed, as I started to go I saw this guy on the sidewalk and I told my wife, "That's my buddy, and I'm going to see him, I don't give a damn about traffic." Cars were parallel parked along the roadside, but I saw enough of an opening between two cars to squeeze angled into, so I turned onto the sidewalk with the back of my car sticking out into road, but I didn't care. I hollered at my friend and when he came up he recognized me and we talked a long time.

I also mentioned early in my story about how my birth certificate got mixed up by the old country doctor with that of the Owens girl. Well, this doctor had a son, and I ran into him at the Prestonsburg unemployment office, and when I first saw him I thought he looked familiar.

"Excuse me," I asked, "but where do you live?"

"Greenup County."

"Where does your dad live?"

"Near Ashland," he replied.

"Was he ever a doctor in Royalton?" I continued questioning.

"Yes."

"I thought I recognized you. You know, your dad brought me into this world."

"What's your name?" he asked.

"James Rudd. You might remember me as Melvin."

"Oh yeah," he answered. "I do."

"Your dad set my left leg when I broke it, too. I think I might have been five or six, a little bit before my dad moved us to Michigan."

"I remember that, too," he replied.

James laughed as he looked at me. I cussed while he was setting it, I sure remember that. I was playing in a little wagon near our house and ran off the side of the hill. Well, at the bottom there was a creek where there was a dynamited dirt road. Yep, I took off over that hill and straight down into that creek. That old dirt road with its rock bed didn't feel so good when I came to a sudden stop. James laughed again.

Another person I crossed paths with was CPT Morris; I was his driver for a bit in Japan, and then we both went to Korea. He got shot the day before I was sent to Japan, and so I wound up seeing him again in the hospital there. But after that time period, I didn't see him again until a few years ago at a 1st Cavalry Division reunion.

"Haven't seen you in a long time," I said.

"Sure haven't. How have you been?"

We caught up a little bit and then I asked him about the mortar platoon.

"SGT Rudd," he said, "there's just me and four men out of that platoon left."

"What happened?"

He had a pained look on his face as he continued. "We were at a location where we had our ammo stored on top of the ground, and the North Koreans managed to get a direct hit with one of their rounds, and the explosion killed all but us few."

"So the mortar platoon was …" I paused a moment.

"Destroyed again," he finished.

64. Reunited with Manring

Let me tell you something that happened a while back. For years, I thought my buddy Roy Manring had died, and then I got word that he was still alive. So I looked him up and placed a call through to his house. When he answered, I didn't think it sounded like him, at least the way I remembered him, and so I asked, "Is this Roy Manring?"

"Yes," he said kind of hesitating.

"Was you in Korea?" When he replied 'yes' again, I asked, "Was you wounded?"

"Yes."

"What color was your hair? And, how much did you weigh?"

"Red hair, 118 pounds. Who is this?"

"Melvin Rudd, from Salyersville, Kentucky."

"Look," he almost hollered, "Don't mess with me. Melvin Rudd is dead!"

"No, this is me," I said.

"No," Manring insisted, "They told me all of you were dead; that I was the sole survivor."

"Well," I answered. "Let me tell you this. Remember

the night before we went to Korea when we went to the club, and then on back to that house with those girls?"

James grinned as he looked at me. I told Manring a few of the specific details of what happened that night, but I really don't want to repeat them here. Anyway, I heard him tell his wife, "Honey, pack a bag. Tomorrow we are going to Salyersville, Kentucky!" And he came.

Let me tell you something, our eyes weren't dry when we greeted each other, and shared our memories of the massacre. It was like being reunited with a long-lost brother, actually with what we went through, he is closer than a brother. We had a nice get-together, and caught up on everything going on in our lives since Korea. Roy didn't know there'd been a total of five of us survive, and that three of us were still alive. Freddie Ryan was living in Cincinnati and so we called him, and he and Manring talked for quite a time.

Manring told me he had been shot thirteen times and spent a total of eighteen months in hospitals in Korea, Japan, and the United States.

"James," he said. "For the longest time, I tried to forget about all the garbage we went through over there. My wife was the only person I even mentioned anything to. Let me ask you this," he asked. "Do you ever feel guilty about being alive?"

"Every damn day," I told him. "It just doesn't seem right, me being here with a job and a family and a nice home, and all our buddies died in that ditch so long ago."

"I have dreams about them all the time, James. I feel guilty that I survived. It's just not right."

And, something else, months later, we were able to get up with Freddie Ryan, and in a nice ceremony we were finally awarded the Prisoner of War medal, and they said a lot of other nice things about us. Better late than never, I guess.

65. My Stepmother, Goldie

I can't remember if I told you that a while after my mother died, my dad remarried, and I didn't always get along the best with his new wife, Goldie. There were probably a dozen things that entered in, perhaps the biggest being I was a mischievous rascal, but the truth is, we didn't always hit it off. Well, some years back, Goldie called me and said she was real sick.

"I'm sorry to hear that," I told her.

"I can hardly move around, James. I can barely get off the couch."

"Again, I really hate that for you."

"James," she said, "there is something I need to talk to you about; something I need for you to do for me."

I wondered what she could possibly need from me as I asked her, "What is it, Goldie?"

"James, I need to apologize for the way I sometimes treated you, years ago, and I need you to forgive me."

"Goldie, I let all that go long ago; you're forgiven."

"Are you sure, James?"

"I'm sure. I forgive you."

"Thank you so much, James. I really need to hear that from you. I was so wrong."

We talked some more, and finally ended our conversation. I'm glad she called me. I'm really glad I was able to let Goldie know I forgave her, because you see, Goldie died that evening. She must have had some kind of premonition or something, and she just wanted to make sure she had a clear conscience before she went.

I've thought about that incident, and I believe it's important to do your best to stand before your God with a clear conscience. That's easier said than done, you know, when you have so many things you wish you could have done differently, but we still have to try; we have to try.

66. Closure

In the end, I have to say there are three people that it is hard to distinguish their importance to me in my life; Flora Sue, my mother, and my dad.

Now I know this would never happen, but if I had them all with me right now, and the good Lord came by and told me I could save one to stay with me, and the other two would have to go, I would have to save Flora Sue, I sure would. I mean, it would be tough saying goodbye to the others again, but Flora is who I would love to have back by my side again, she sure is.

Now I know you can't go back and change things, but there is a regret I have. I have always regretted taking the orders I considered a mistake, what I perceived as coming from a green, hard-headed Lieutenant. He should have listened more to the people under him, but he didn't seem to think that younger enlisted men had anything to say to him.

Now I know I wasn't the perfect father myself, but if I have anything to say to parents today, it is that maybe they should try to teach their kids more about not talking back to those in authority, to have more respect, and to

teach them obedience. That doesn't mean to blindly follow, but do learn how to follow instructions. Teach them
to show more respect for other peoples' property.

And for children, some need to learn to be thank-
ful for what they have, not complaining about what they
don't have. They may not have a whole lot, but the parents may be doing the best they can at the time.

You know, my perspective has changed over the years.
When I went back to Korea the second time, I was still
just so mad and full of bitterness and the desire for revenge. Looking back, and thinking about what Jesus said
in what we know as the Golden Rule, there's no way I
would ever want to be treated the way I wanted to treat
North Koreans when I went back. But I was so bitter
over Hill 303 and the way it all happened, that for a
long time I couldn't stand North Koreans, any of them.
But over the years, with the help of Flora Sue, God, and
thinking a lot about the things Mom and Dad taught
me, I've come to realize they were just doing the job they
were told to do, and I was wrong in my bitterness and hatred. I guess with time, healing does come.

"James," I said, "I need to ask you a question."

"Go ahead," he replied.

"Well," I asked, "if a North Korean nurse started
working here at Mountain Manor, and they brought her
into the room here and said she was your nurse, would
you let her take care of you?"

James looked down, brought his hands up so they
were folded over his stomach, and pursed his lips. He
looked back at me, and then cocked his head a bit sideways to the left. He slowly nodded his head as he quietly and thoughtfully said, "Yes, she could treat me." He

looked down again, then back up, took a deep breath, and repeated himself, "She could treat me."

About the Author

Basil B. Clark is a retired associate professor from the University of Pikeville (KY) where he taught theatre and communication courses. He currently serves as a volunteer mentor and instructor at Walker State Prison in Rock Spring, GA, the state's first totally Faith and Character-based prison program. Basil and his wife Cora reside near Chattanooga, Tennessee.

CPSIA information can be obtained
at www.ICGtesting.com
Printed in the USA
BVHW04s2351160418
513501BV00005B/610/P